BABE RUTH

UP*close:*

BABE RUTH

a twentieth-century life by
WILBORN HAMPTON

VIKING

VIKING
Published by Penguin Group
Penguin Young Readers Group, 345 Hudson Street, New York, New York 10014, U.S.A.
Penguin Group (Canada), 90 Eglinton Avenue East, Suite 700, Toronto, Ontario,
Canada M4P 2Y3 (a division of Pearson Penguin Canada Inc.)
Penguin Books Ltd, 80 Strand, London WC2R 0RL, England
Penguin Ireland, 25 St Stephen's Green, Dublin 2, Ireland (a division of Penguin Books Ltd)
Penguin Group (Australia), 250 Camberwell Road, Camberwell, Victoria 3124, Australia
(a division of Pearson Australia Group Pty Ltd)
Penguin Books India Pvt Ltd, 11 Community Centre, Panchsheel Park, New Delhi – 110 017, India
Penguin Group (NZ), 67 Apollo Drive, Rosedale, North Shore 0632, New Zealand
(a division of Pearson New Zealand Ltd)
Penguin Books (South Africa) (Pty) Ltd, 24 Sturdee Avenue, Rosebank, Johannesburg 2196,
South Africa

Penguin Books Ltd, Registered Offices: 80 Strand, London WC2R 0RL, England

First published in 2009 by Viking, a division of Penguin Young Readers Group

10 9 8 7 6 5 4 3 2 1

Photo credits can be found on page 205.

LIBRARY OF CONGRESS CATALOGING-IN-PUBLICATION DATA
Hampton, Wilborn.
Up close, Babe Ruth : a twentieth-century life / by Wilborn Hampton.
p. cm.—(Up close)
Includes bibliographical references and index.
ISBN 978-0-670-06305-5 (hardcover)
1. Ruth, Babe, 1895–1948. 2. Baseball players—United States—Biography. I. Title.
GV865.R8H36 2009
796.357092—dc22
[B]
2008021550

Printed in the U.S.A.
Set in Goudy
Book design by Jim Hoover

For Mickey and Alan Friedman
and
Jim and Becky Rebhorn
Bleacher Buddies for life

BABE RUTH

CONTENTS

FOREWORD

EVERY KID WHO ever picked up a baseball knows the name Babe Ruth. Even those who are not quite sure what records he held or what he did to achieve them know that the Babe was considered the best ever to play the game. Around the world, even in countries where baseball is not played, people know that Babe Ruth was the epitome of excellence.

Few, however, know who the man behind the legend really was. They know he was the home-run king, the Bambino, the Sultan of Swat. But the story of who he was before he became all those things is clouded in mystery and has been sugarcoated by generations of sportswriters and fans. As a result, there are probably more stories about Babe Ruth than about any other sports figure of the twentieth century. It was widely reported, for example, that he was an orphan who was determined to find his way out of poverty through baseball. The truth, as always, is more complicated.

George Herman Ruth was not an orphan. He was a bad kid from a bad neighborhood whose parents placed him in a Catholic reform school for delinquents and orphans at the age of seven. He discovered baseball almost by chance because one of the Xaverian Brothers who ran the school thought it could help him straighten out his life, and little George fell in love with the game. In fact, nobody loved the game more and nobody played it better.

As a boy growing up, I played a lot of baseball on vacant lots or school playgrounds with my neighborhood friends. We used book satchels or rocks or whatever we could find for bases, and we rarely had more than one ball and one bat and half a dozen gloves to share for both sides. Although all of my friends had favorite players from major-league teams (mine was Willie Mays of the then New York Giants), the one player who was regarded by everyone as the all-time greatest was Babe Ruth.

Although I soon realized I was not going to be a

professional baseball player, my love of the game and my fascination with the Babe only grew. His ghost haunted baseball season after season. He remained the standard against which all players who followed him were measured. Who was the boy who fought his way out of a Baltimore slum to become the idol of every kid in America?

The only way to find an answer was to write his life story. In the process I discovered a man who lived hard and played hard and who was even bigger than his myth.

Babe Ruth at batting practice in 1927. He copied his famous swing from Brother Matthias at St. Mary's in Baltimore.

INTRODUCTION

ON FEBRUARY 14, 1914, George Ruth was outside St. Mary's Industrial School for Boys in Baltimore, on one of the school's two playgrounds, when a big limousine drove through the main gates.

It was cold that St. Valentine's Day. It had been snowing, and the Big Yard, as the playing field for the older boys at St. Mary's was known, was icy and slippery. With no organized sport planned for their recreation period on that frosty day, George, who had just turned twenty the week before, and several of the other boys were running and sliding on the frozen turf, killing time until they had to go back inside. They noticed the big car as it drove up to the front entrance of the school, but it didn't stop their frolicking on the ice.

Inside the car were three men—Fritz Maisel, a native of Baltimore who played baseball for the New

York Yankees and who owned the car; Brother Gilbert, the baseball coach at St. Joseph's, a neighboring Roman Catholic school and a rival of St. Mary's; and Jack Dunn, the owner of the Baltimore Orioles, then a minor-league team. They got out and went into the building.

Two of the men were there on a mission. Dunn was looking for a pitcher for his baseball team, which was scheduled to start spring training in a couple of weeks. Brother Gilbert wanted to make sure Dunn didn't steal his own ace left-hander at St. Joseph's. Maisel was basically along for the ride, especially since it was his car.

Dunn had first heard about George Ruth from a friend named Joe Engel, a former player for the Washington Senators who had seen George pitch for St. Mary's in a school exhibition game. Then Dunn heard the same name from Brother Gilbert when he went to scout a possible pitcher at St. Joseph's. Brother Gilbert, wanting to keep his own player in school and pitching for St. Joseph's, began to extol the natural talent of a kid named Ruth over at St. Mary's. Dunn decided it was time to see for himself.

The trio first went to the office of Brother Paul, who was the superintendent of the school, and chatted while they waited for Brother Matthias, a huge yet soft-spoken man who stood six foot six, weighed 250 pounds, and was St. Mary's physical-education director. Dunn learned from Brother Paul that George's father was still alive, but that the school had legal responsibility for his affairs until he was twenty-one.

When Brother Matthias joined them, Dunn asked him whether the boy could play ball.

"Ruth can hit," Brother Matthias said, never one to elaborate.

"Can he pitch?" Dunn persisted. After all, Dunn was in the market for a pitcher.

"Sure," Brother Matthias replied vaguely. "He can do anything."

Dunn decided he wasn't going to get much more information out of Brother Matthias and asked to see George. They found him on the Big Yard, wearing overalls, and Dunn asked someone to find a baseball.

Brother Gilbert began to get nervous. He knew Dunn wanted a pitcher, and he had touted this George Ruth as a terrific pitching prospect. But the truth was that Brother Gilbert had never seen George pitch. In fact, the only time he had seen George play was in one game between St. Mary's and St. Joseph's, which St. Mary's had won 6–0. In that game, George had played catcher.

There are various accounts of what exactly took place on that cold day in February 1914. In a ghost-written 1928 autobiography titled *Babe Ruth's Own Book of Baseball*, Ruth said Dunn "had me pitch to him for a half hour I guess, talking to me all the time, and telling me not to strain and not to try too hard."

At the end of it, Dunn and the other men went back into the school office, and a short time later they sent for young George. Dunn didn't waste any time.

"How about it, young man, do you want to play baseball?" he asked George.

George didn't even pause to think.

"Sure," he said, laughing. "I'll play. When do I start?"

Brother Gilbert felt he should explain all the ramifications to George. He pointed out that while the school was still his official guardian, Dunn now would become his acting guardian until George turned twenty-one, which at the time was the age of legal adulthood. George also was told that he would be paid $600 for a six-month season, or about $25 a week. To George, who suddenly realized they were serious, but also had never contemplated actually being paid to play baseball, it seemed like a fortune. Dunn had a contract with him and George signed it immediately. He raced out of the room to tell the other boys.

When his teammates heard the news that George would be leaving in two weeks to play baseball with the Baltimore Orioles, they were happy for him that he was free of St. Mary's. But a group of them who had been waiting outside Brother Paul's office shouted in unison, "There goes our ball club."

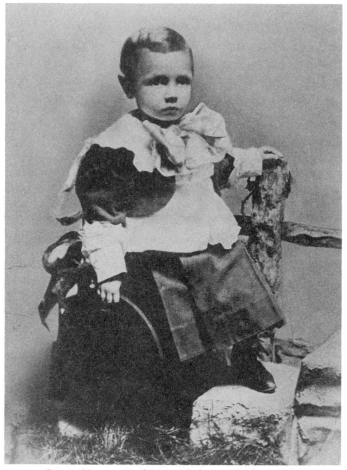

George Herman Ruth Jr. in a baby picture from 1898.
For much of his life he wasn't sure of the exact year of his birth.

ONE

THE ONLY THING anyone knows for certain about Babe Ruth's early childhood is that it was bad. Ruth was the first to admit it. In his autobiography, titled *The Babe Ruth Story*, written in 1948 with the sportswriter Bob Considine, Ruth began with the simple statement: "I was a bad kid."

The details of that childhood, however, are at best sketchy, relying on hazy memory and anecdote to back up many of the claims and stories. During his life and after his death, so much was written about Babe Ruth that it is hard to know what is real and what is myth. Babe himself was sometimes unreliable, saying one thing at one time and another thing later. With so few facts to go on, writers often tend to make up some details, and, as always when stories are repeated, there is a lot of exaggeration. It was confidently reported, for example, that the Babe was an orphan. Or that his name wasn't even Ruth. There was even confusion over when he was born.

Throughout most of his life, Ruth thought he was born on February 7, 1894, and he always celebrated his birthday on that date. Yet in 1934, when he applied for a passport to travel to Japan on his first trip outside North America, the copy of his birth certificate that was sent to him from Baltimore said he was born on February 6, 1895. Ruth ignored the new date and continued to celebrate his birthday on February 7. As for the discrepancy in the year, he would say, "What difference does it make?"

Whatever the date, he was born in his maternal grandfather's house on Emory Street in Baltimore. His father was George Herman Ruth Sr., and his mother was the former Catherine Schamberger, sometimes spelled Katherine, who was called Kate or Katie. Poor people in those days couldn't afford to have children delivered in a hospital, and the Ruth family certainly couldn't. As Babe wrote later: "We were poor. Very poor." So the birth took place at home with the assistance of a midwife named Minnie Graf.

Babe's father had held an assortment of jobs around Baltimore. At one time, he was a lightning-rod salesman, peddling the gadgets that people attached to the roofs of their houses that were supposed to prevent lightning from striking them and starting a fire. Later, he was a horse driver, a streetcar brakeman, and a bartender, working in several waterfront taverns. He moved his family often in the early years. He finally ended up owning his own saloon at 426 West Camden Street, near the Baltimore docks.

The family history of Ruth's mother is even more vague. In one group photo, taken at what appears to be a family or neighborhood picnic, she is one of dozens of people in the picture, a young woman in a white dress with her hair done up in a bun, looking sternly at the camera. Ruth always said that his mother was "mainly Irish." Schamberger, however, is hardly an Irish name, and her father originally came from Germany. Even her maiden name is variously spelled as Schaumberger, or, as Ruth himself spelled it in his book, Schanberger. It could be that one of Kate's parents or grandparents had been Irish, but the Ruths spoke German at home, and young George grew up speaking both German and English.

There is even a dispute over his religious background. It was generally assumed that both Ruth's mother and father had been Lutherans, as most German Americans were. Other reports said that his mother was Roman Catholic, which would support the Irish connection, and his father was Lutheran. Records at St. Mary's agreed with that and noted that Ruth was baptized Catholic when he was one month old. However, he was baptized again years later, and the baptismal certificate then said he was "a convert."

The truth is that neither of his parents was a regular churchgoer, and George Ruth and Katie Schamberger were married in a Baptist church and ended up living in an apartment over the saloon Ruth senior owned.

Katie bore eight children in all, including two sets of twins. Six of them died, either in childbirth or in infancy. Infant mortality was not uncommon then. Although he once said he had an older brother who died, George was actually the firstborn and he was named after his father. Throughout his childhood, he was known in the family as Little George and his father as Big George.

The only other surviving child, born in 1900, five years after Little George, was a girl named Mary Margaret, who was always called Mamie. She was one of those two sets of twins, and she lived to be ninety-one, dying in 1992. In later years, she became a source of family history for many writers and biographers trying to piece together a picture of the Babe's youth, but her memory was not always reliable. For example, she insisted her parents were "in the restaurant business," rather then proprietors of a seedy tavern. Mamie and her brother were never close, and as Babe once said in talking about his childhood, "I hardly knew my parents."

A true picture of Babe's childhood, therefore, is at best obscure. Babe himself was not above adding to the uncertainty about his early years. For example, when it was first reported that his family name was not Ruth after all, but Erhardt—or, as others had it, Gerhardt—he kept the controversy going. When a reporter commented on the similarity of his new last name of Erhardt to that of a Brooklyn Dodger player named Ehrhardt, Ruth said with a straight face, "mine has only one 'h.'"

It was enough to keep the misinformation alive, and even *The New York Times*, in an article late in his life, referred to him as George Herman Erhardt Ruth. Later, both he and Mamie categorically denied that Erhardt or Gerhardt was any part of their name.

Almost from the time he could walk, Ruth was constantly in trouble. For one thing, he had little supervision at home. His mother was frail and frequently ill. She seemed constantly to be either expecting a baby or grieving over the death of one. When she died at the age of thirty-eight, when George was seventeen years old, the death certificate listed the cause as "exhaustion." At any rate, his mother was not much of a presence in George's life, and he was told not to make demands on her because of her delicate condition.

Ruth's father spent almost every waking moment tending his bar and grocery store. He opened it early in the morning, and he kept it open far into the night. He was a big burly man who seemed to have a cigar in his mouth at all times and was almost always angry, always working, and always worried about making ends meet and paying the bills. As a result, Big George had no time for Little George either, and kept telling him to go outside and play.

Adding to the lack of parental supervision, another problem was that the neighborhood itself was no place for a boy to grow up in. Camden Street in those days was in one of the roughest parts of the city. The general area was referred to by residents of Baltimore as "Pigtown," because pigs were often herded through its streets on their way to a slaughterhouse that was located nearby. It was in the waterfront district, and the only playgrounds Little George knew were the narrow streets and alleys around the dockyards, which were crowded with sailors, stevedores, prostitutes, and petty thieves.

Recreation for young George and the other kids he grew up around consisted of taunting drunken sailors or pilfering fruit from street shops. One pastime was to throw stolen tomatoes or eggs at the trucks and wagons that came to the docks to pick up the goods brought in on ships that arrived from overseas. Years later, Babe jokingly said he first learned to control his pitches by throwing rotten fruit and eggs at the horse-drawn trucks around the Baltimore docks. The truck drivers would often lash out at the kids on the street with their whips.

George was no stranger to whippings at home, either. His father beat him often when he would get into trouble, and he wrote later that his father even turned a horsewhip on him on occasion. There were frequent run-ins with the police, as well, and every time a policeman brought him home, he was sure to get another whipping there.

In order to survive in such surroundings, Little George and the other boys had to create their own aura of toughness. George learned the lessons of the street quickly. He was a big boy with a moon face, a flat nose, large lips, and small eyes that took in everything he saw. There were always fights breaking out in the streets around the dockyards, and the example set for George from a young age was that disagreements were settled with one's fists.

By the turn of the twentieth century, baseball had already become America's national pastime, and

Little George and his friends played some version of it in the streets around the docks, although they rarely had real bats, balls, and gloves.

By the time he was old enough to start school, Little George's contempt for authority was already deeply ingrained. He almost never attended school, and he was frequently caught by truant officers and brought home. Each time, his father would give him a beating and tell him that he had to go to school. Each time, George would endure the punishment and ignore the admonition.

It wasn't that he occasionally played hooky. He simply refused to go to school. With his mother always ill and often confined to bed and his father running a saloon, there was no one to make George go to school. So he didn't. From a young age, he had begun to sip beer or even whiskey left in glasses at the bar or on the tables in his father's saloon. He started chewing tobacco. He had been caught stealing, and his run-ins with the police were becoming more frequent.

Things came to a crisis on the morning of Friday, June 13, 1902, when George Ruth Senior packed a bag with his son's clothes in it and took him on the Wilkins Avenue trolley to a stop nearly at the end of the line. Their destination was the St. Mary's Industrial School for Boys, an institution for homeless, impoverished, or delinquent boys that was run by a Roman Catholic order known as the Xaverian Brothers.

There has been a lot of speculation about what was the final straw that led his parents to take their son to St. Mary's. Babe's sister, Mamie, said it was only because he wouldn't go to school. But Mamie was just two years old at the time, and her memory always found the rosiest version of their childhood. There was one report that a pistol had been fired during a fight in his father's saloon, and when a neighbor complained, the Baltimore juvenile authorities ruled that a saloon was no place to bring up a child and ordered him taken to St. Mary's. Another account said that his mother had become more seriously ill, and his father could not be responsible for him. The only reason given on the admission papers at St. Mary's was that he was "incorrigible."

He was seven years old.

Whatever the reason, Little George only stayed for a month the first time he was enrolled there. According to school records, and Babe's own account, he returned home in July 1902, only to be returned to St. Mary's in November. His parents moved to a new apartment just before Christmas that year, and he again joined them. He lived with his parents for just over a year but was sent back to St. Mary's in 1904. For most of the rest of his childhood—except for a couple of other times on "parole," as Babe called his periods away from the school—St. Mary's was his home.

From the start at St. Mary's, Little George was taught to read and write. The purpose of the school, however, was also to teach the disadvantaged boys in its care the skills that would help them find a useful life for themselves. George took classes in tailoring and shirtmaking, and throughout his time there it was assumed that when he finally left at the age of twenty-one, he would be qualified to find a job as a tailor.

The main skill that Little George learned at St. Mary's, however, was how to swing a baseball bat. And the man he had to thank for that—and did, throughout his life—was a member of the Xaverian Order known as Brother Matthias.

TWO

BROTHER MATTHIAS WAS born Martin L. Boutlier on July 11, 1872, at Lingan, Cape Breton, Canada. He was an extremely well-coordinated and athletic child and grew into a giant of a young man. Yet for all his imposing physical appearance, he was a mild-mannered, soft-spoken, and patient man who walked with a shambling gait and who ran with small, pigeon-toed steps.

By all accounts, he could have had a notable career in sports himself. By his teens, however, he felt he had a vocation, and he began a period of religious training with a relatively new order of Catholic brothers known as the Xaverians. Upon finishing his noviceship he took the name Brother Matthias, and in 1894 he was assigned to St. Mary's Industrial School for Boys in Baltimore.

St. Mary's had been built nearly three decades earlier, in 1866, primarily as a home to care for boys whose fathers had been killed in the Civil War, which had ended only the preceding year. Over the years it had expanded to include orphans, delinquents, and troubled boys who were at risk. The school was run by the Congregation of the Brothers of Francis Xavier, an order of Catholic brothers founded by Theodore James Rijken in Belgium in 1839. Although the brothers were not priests, they were more than laymen. They wore long black cassocks; took vows of poverty, chastity, and obedience; and were dedicated to teaching youth.

By the time little George Ruth came through its doors, St. Mary's had become a well-known institution in Baltimore. Located on the outskirts of the city, it was a large and imposing edifice, five stories tall, surrounded by open space. The Wilkins Avenue trolley stopped right in front of its gates. As you stepped off the streetcar and walked up the long drive that led to it, the building looked like a hospital, or even a prison. The main entrance was in a sort of tower, with wings running out on either side. A chapel, as big as some cathedrals, was at one end.

There were about eight hundred boys at St. Mary's when George first went there, and at the age of seven he was among the youngest. The school was divided into dormitories, and George was assigned to one of them. Each dorm had rows of beds, and with each bed there was one chair. Showers and toilets were adjacent to each dorm, and meals were taken by all the boys in one huge dining hall. The school was run along almost military lines, with strict rules about talking during meals or after lights-out, which came at eight P.M. every night. One brother was assigned to each dorm, and he would often tell the boys a story at bedtime before retiring to his own private room at one end of the dorm, with a glass window in the door so he could keep an eye on them.

Wake-up each morning was at six A.M., and a chapel service started each day. A boy did not have to be from a Catholic family to be taken in, and although attendance at chapel was mandatory and there were classes offered in religion, there was no pressure on non-Catholics to convert. Apart from the Babe, for example, another of St. Mary's famous graduates was Al Jolsen, the singer and movie star, who was Jewish.

Breakfast was usually oatmeal, and classes began

immediately after. Ruth and the other younger boys were taught the basic three Rs. Lunch was usually soup and bread, which was baked at the school by boys in the kitchen. After a brief recess, classes resumed. These, however, were vocational rather than scholastic, and boys were assigned to certain training programs for which the brothers determined each had the most aptitude. There were classes in tailoring, shoemaking, carpentry, gardening, farming, baking— almost any trade that a boy might pursue to earn a living once he became an adult and left the school.

Supper each night was again usually a soup or stew, with more of the school-baked bread. Sometimes in the evening there also would be bologna, and once a week, the boys were treated to hot dogs. Then they would be back in their dorms by eight P.M.

Between the end of each day's classes and supper, however, the boys had a couple of hours of physical exercise outside. The recreation areas were divided into the Big Yard for older boys and the Little Yard for the younger ones, and each yard had its playing fields. The boys went outside even in winter. They played football, basketball, soccer, volleyball. Races were also organized, and boxing matches. But by far the favorite sport was baseball, and that was what the boys played from March until well into October.

Brother Matthias's primary job at St. Mary's was to be in charge of discipline, no small feat for one man in a school of eight hundred boys, many of whom were there precisely for their disregard for any kind of discipline. As athletic director, he also organized each dorm into baseball teams, and the teams were arranged in leagues. All the boys played baseball. There were as many as forty teams of different age brackets among the students at the school. In addition to supervising the baseball program, Brother Matthias coached a sort of all-star team of the school's best players, and St. Mary's competed against other schools during the season.

If anything, Brother Matthias's own prowess with a bat and a baseball made him an authority figure for the boys as much as his imposing presence. One of the Saturday evening attractions at the school featured Brother Matthias hitting fungoes, tossing up ball after ball with one hand and then belting them high, high into the air and far, far into the field. All the boys would race into the yard to watch him. Ruth recalled his own memory of Brother Matthias's Saturday exhibitions in *The Babe Ruth Story*.

"I think I was born as a hitter the first day I ever saw him hit a baseball. I can remember it as if it were yesterday. It was during the summer of 1902, my first year in St. Mary's," Ruth wrote.

Brother Matthias would stand at the end of the yard, a finger mitt on his left hand and a bat in his right, toss the ball up with his left hand and give it a terrific belt with the bat he held in his right hand. When he felt like it he could hit it a little harder and make the ball clear the fence in center field. It would have to carry at least 350 feet. . . . I would just stand there and watch him, bug-eyed. I had never seen anything like that in my life, nor anyone who was even close to Brother Matthias when it came to manliness, kindness and grace.

Whether it was because George was the youngest among the boys or because he saw the potential for greatness in him, Brother Matthias took a special interest in little George almost from the time he first entered St. Mary's.

During his first summer there, he was assigned to

Babe learned to play baseball at St. Mary's Industrial School and was the star of his dorm team.

his dorm's young boys' team. Brother Herman was his first coach, and he gave George a mitt and told him to try catching with it. It was the first time George had ever played with a real baseball glove. He was left-handed, so he put the mitt on his right hand. The mitt, however, was designed to be worn on the left hand, for a right-handed thrower. So he began his career as a catcher by wearing his mitt on the wrong hand.

Later on, he would learn to wear the mitt on his left hand. He would catch the ball, pull off the glove, and then toss the ball back to the pitcher with his left hand.

George loved to catch, and later, he loved to pitch. From the time he first touched a baseball at St. Mary's he loved the feel of it in his hands. He loved to catch sharp, fast balls in a mitt, and he loved to wait under high fly balls until they dropped into his glove. He loved to throw hard balls ninety feet from the mound to the plate, and he loved to hurl the ball with all his might from the outfield. But even more than he loved to pitch and catch baseballs, he loved to bat.

From the first moment he stepped onto a baseball diamond, he was a natural. It wasn't long before he was playing on teams with boys three and four years older than he. Brother Albin was his next coach, but by this time Brother Matthias had noticed his ability and would give George extra training, spending hours hitting him grounders and pop-ups to improve his fielding. Through his years at St. Mary's, George would play every position on the diamond, but whether he wore the mitt on his right hand or left hand, he was always regarded primarily as a catcher in the beginning.

The story of how Ruth came to be a pitcher began

as a sort of punishment handed out by Brother Matthias. When he was about fifteen years old, he was the catcher in a game in which the St. Mary's school team was playing another school, and they were getting beat badly. Brother Matthias, who was the coach, had changed pitchers a couple of times, but the other team kept piling up runs. George, who was always a fierce competitor, started laughing and made a few derogatory comments from behind the plate to his own pitcher. Brother Matthias called a time-out and walked over to the catcher's box.

"What are you laughing at, George?" Ruth recalled him asking.

"That guy out there—he's getting his brains knocked out," George replied, continuing to laugh at the ineptitude of the team's latest pitcher.

He recalled that Brother Matthias looked at him for a long time.

"All right, George, *you* pitch," Brother Matthias finally said.

George stopped laughing.

"I never pitched in my life," George protested. "I can't pitch."

"Oh, you must know a lot about it," Brother

Matthias said. "You know enough to know your friend isn't any good. So go ahead out there and show us how it's done."

George knew Brother Matthias wasn't joking, so he left his catcher's mask and mitt on the bench, got a fielder's glove, and went out to the mound. He didn't even know how to stand on the rubber. And he had never attempted to throw a curve ball in his life.

Even though he may not have saved the game for St. Mary's that day, George felt a strange attraction to the pitcher's mound. As he put it in his autobiography, "I felt, somehow, as if I had been born out there and that this was a kind of home for me." As he did with every other position he played on the field, George worked at learning to be a pitcher. He threw hard and fast and labored over controlling his pitches and developing a curve ball. During his last two seasons at St. Mary's, Brother Matthias used him often as a pitcher. Sometimes he would start George as a pitcher, then move him to another position because he didn't want to take George and his bat out of the lineup. Other times, he would start George at catcher, then move him to pitcher in the late innings.

By this time George was the undisputed star of the St. Mary's team. During his last years there, he probably played baseball just about every day during the season at St. Mary's. There are few firsthand accounts of the school games, but those that exist attest to Ruth's all-round ability. For example, one account in the school newspaper of a game in 1912, which would have been his next-to-last year there, had a box score that showed that he played catcher, third base, and pitcher over the nine innings. He hit a double, a triple, and a home run. He also struck out six batters.

Perhaps the most important game he played, however, was one that didn't seem so important at the time. But it certainly had an effect on whether young George Ruth would end up as a tailor or a baseball player.

The Xaverian Brothers ran another school called Mount St. Joseph's that was located not far from St. Mary's. It was regarded as something of a higher class institution, one that the boys at St. Mary's referred to as "the rich school down the road." Oddly enough, the two schools rarely played against each other.

The athletic director and coach of the Mount

St. Joseph's team was Brother Gilbert, who also had a reputation as an expert on baseball talent. One of his players reported to Brother Gilbert about seeing a kid named George Ruth in a game at St. Mary's, saying that he was the best hitter he had ever seen. Brother Gilbert decided to go see this phenomenon himself. One afternoon, he drove over from Mount St. Joe's to see a game at St. Mary's in which the then eighteen-year-old George was playing his usual position as catcher. In an article he wrote later for the *Boston Globe* in 1928, he recalled his visit:

> Clad in a baseball uniform that was a trifle small for him, there strode up to the plate the most graceful of big men that I have ever seen. . . . With a slight manifestation of nervousness the opposing pitcher turned his back to home plate and waved his outfielders back. He need not have done so; they were already on their way.

In his account, Brother Gilbert said the player in right field moved so far back that he was standing in the outfield of another diamond, where another game was taking place. All the players in that game stopped and turned to watch George take his turn at bat. George did not disappoint them. He cracked the first pitch so hard that it flew over the fielder's head and into the adjacent field for a home run.

Like everything else in George Herman Ruth's young life, there are multiple stories about how his talents came to the attention of Brother Gilbert and Jack Dunn, the owner and manager of the Baltimore Orioles. Some versions say that Brother Gilbert had already seen George pitch, when Mount St. Joseph's and St. Mary's played each other in a game in which he struck out 22 batters, winning 6–0. Another version says that Dunn, after hearing about Ruth, went to see him play at the school one afternoon, and was so impressed that he decided to offer him a contract a few months later. But Brother Gilbert said in his own book that he had never seen George pitch when he brought Jack Dunn out to St. Mary's that cold February day in 1914. And Dunn always insisted in later interviews he had never seen George play baseball until he took him to spring training.

There is an account in the St. Mary's school paper of a routine game in late September of 1913—one of the last George played at the school—in which he was the pitcher, when St. Mary's won 6–0. "He also struck out 22 and issued but one pass," the story said. "During the game he hit safely four times." But if that was the same game Brother Gilbert reportedly saw, there is no mention of it being against Mount St. Joseph's, a curious omission if true, since it was St. Mary's archrival.

Whatever the circumstances that led to it, George's time at St. Mary's drew to a close when Brother Gilbert and Jack Dunn met with Brother Paul and Brother Matthias, and signed Ruth to a six-month contract that paid him the small fortune of $600. This was at a time when an entire family could easily live on about $10 a week.

As Ruth became famous, sportswriters scrambled to discover and tell the story of the unknown kid who was taking the game of baseball by storm. Many of those early stories wrongly credited Brother Gilbert with discovering Ruth, being his mentor, and teaching him the game. Even an early book, titled *Babe*

Ruth's Own Book of Baseball, implied that Brother Gilbert was the motivating force behind George's early training at St. Mary's. That book, however, was ghostwritten—probably by Ford Frick, who was then a New York sportswriter—and Ruth probably never read a word of it. Brother Gilbert, however, taught at another school, and while he had the connections that brought Jack Dunn to St. Mary's, the man who made George Herman Ruth the player he became was Brother Matthias.

George copied his swing from the way Brother Matthias used to toss up the ball and hit it with a sweeping, uppercut motion; George learned to run the same way Brother Matthias ran, with small, pigeon-toed steps; George even tried to emulate the quiet humility with which Brother Matthias lived his life. And when George would fall short of that goal in the years to come, as he frequently did, it was always to Brother Matthias he would turn for help. Brother Matthias had faith in George at a time when few people did. And for George, Brother Matthias was quite simply "the greatest man I've ever known."

George stayed at St. Mary's for two more weeks

after signing the contract. On the day he finally left, he packed his few clothes in an old suitcase and was saying his good-byes to a group of other kids and brothers at the front door. Brother Matthias was the last one there. He took George's hand in his own, looked him in the eyes, and said quietly, "You'll make it, George." Then he turned and walked away. And George Herman Ruth walked out of St. Mary's to a life he could not even have imagined a month earlier.

THREE

GEORGE HAD NEVER been on a train before. The plans called for him to report to the Kernan Hotel in Baltimore on Monday afternoon, and then he and the rest of the team would take the train from Union Station that night to travel to Fayetteville, North Carolina, for the start of spring training.

After leaving St. Mary's on Friday, George spent the weekend with his father in his apartment above the saloon, and said good-bye to some of his old friends from Pigtown. If his father had any reaction to George becoming a baseball player, he never expressed it publicly.

On Sunday night, the night before George was to leave, a huge blizzard hit the entire Northeast. Over a foot of snow fell on Baltimore, and high winds had knocked over trees and caused other damage around the city. As a result of the storm, Dunn had to alter his plans. A lot of the players were unable to get to Baltimore in time to take the train to North Carolina. It was doubtful even that the train would be able to depart on schedule.

Young George, however, made his way through the snow-covered city, from the waterfront to the hotel. It had never occurred to him that they might not leave on time. At the hotel he met a few of the other newcomers to the Orioles team, as well as some of the old-timers. One of the other newcomers was Bill Morrisette, the pitcher from Mount St. Joseph's that Dunn had also signed on the recommendation of Brother Gilbert.

Because of the storm interrupting so many players' travel arrangements, Dunn decided to send to North Carolina the players who were already there. But he would stay in Baltimore several days and come down later with the rest of the team.

If George was the most excited of the players to board the train, he was also the most gullible. The others quickly realized that George, who was nineteen but thought he was twenty, was a real greenhorn who had never traveled anywhere except on a street-car, and they played an old trick on him.

Sleeping cars on trains were divided into upper and lower berths, and George was assigned one of the upper bunks. In each upper bunk, a little string hammocklike storage rack ran the length of the berth for the occupant to put his clothes in. One of the players told George that it was actually there for baseball pitchers to rest their arm in while they slept. Throughout the night, George hardly slept a wink, trying to keep his arm suspended in the little hammock hanging at the side of the bed. When the train pulled into Fayetteville the next morning, George's arm was stiff and sore, and he almost began his professional career on the disabled list.

The snowstorm that had devastated the Northeast had brought heavy rains as far south as North Caro-lina, and as the players checked into the Lafayette Hotel, it seemed they would not be able to practice for days. The rains continued on and off through most of the first week of spring training, and about the only baseball they could play were games of catch at the town's Fair Grounds or indoors at the local armory.

George, however, was having a great time, even if he couldn't play ball. It was all new to him. One of the most fascinating things for him was the elevator at the hotel. He had never ridden on an elevator, either, and to the amusement of the other players, he would spend hours just riding the elevator up and down, from the hotel's top floor to the lobby. He even gave the elevator operator some money to let him run it.

From his years at St. Mary's, George was used to getting up by dawn, and it was a habit that would take time to break. He would get up in Fayetteville at five or six A.M., and head out to the streets, just walking around the town until the hotel restaurant opened for breakfast. His favorite walk was to the train station. He adored the trains, and he would spend the early morning just watching them pull into the station and leave again.

He was usually back by the time the restaurant opened. For most of his life, George's diet had consisted of oatmeal for breakfast and soup and bread for lunch and dinner. Now, with a menu full of options before him, George ate like a horse.

At first, his only constraint was money. Although George wouldn't receive his first paycheck until the end of the month, Jack Dunn had given him five dollars for spending money before he left Baltimore. It was the most money George had ever had in his life, but at his first breakfast in the hotel he was trying to figure out how to make it last until he got paid. As he was looking over the choices, another player told him to order anything he wanted because the team paid for all meals during spring training.

"You mean I can eat anything I want, and it won't cost me anything?" he asked. Assured that the club picked up the bill for meals, George ended up eating three orders of wheat cakes and three side orders of ham. When he finally looked up he saw several of the other players just watching him in amazement. George just laughed.

"A guy's got to be strong to play ball," he said.

Ruth's eating habits became legendary. Former teammates told stories about how he once ate a three-pound steak covered in chili sauce, or an eighteen-egg omelet for breakfast, or a whole pie for dessert. Maybe it was because he was perpetually hungry after years of meager rations at St. Mary's, but he ate as if every meal were his last. And it wasn't just at mealtimes that he stuffed himself. He often ate during games. He would send the bat boy out for hot dogs between innings, and sometimes ate three or four during a game. As he got older, Ruth's appetite would affect his playing as he battled weight problems. But in the dawn of his career, his eating was more a source of awe than concern.

It wasn't until Saturday, at the end of their first week of training camp, that the Orioles finally were able to hold a real practice session. Dunn still had not arrived, but most of the team was there by then, and Ben Egan, the Orioles' catcher and captain, organized a seven-inning intra-squad game to be played at the Fayetteville Fair Grounds.

The teams were called the Buzzards and the Sparrows, and George Ruth started as shortstop for the Buzzards, batting fifth. The Buzzards scored a run in the top of the first inning, but George, in his first trip to the plate, made an out. The Sparrows came back with a run of their own to tie the game in the bottom of the first.

In the top of the second, the Buzzards managed to

*Ruth began his baseball career as a catcher,
the position he played for his team at St. Mary's.*

load the bases, and Egan hit a double, scoring three runs. The next batter got a single, and George came up for the second time, with two men on base. The pitcher for the Sparrows delivered a ball over the middle of the plate, and George twisted his body around in a backswing and hit it with all his might. Those who saw it would never forget it the rest of their lives.

The ball kept going and going and going. The

right fielder for the Sparrows was Morrisette, the recruit from St. Joseph's. The ball went over his head, over the fence, beyond a track that ran around the ballpark, and landed in a cornfield. Before Morrisette could retrieve the ball, George walked around the bases for his first home run in his first game as a professional ballplayer. The fans in the stands and the players on the field just watched in awe. The ball traveled so far they marked the spot it landed and measured it—428 feet. For years, the locals in Fayetteville had talked about a homer once hit by Jim Thorpe, the Olympic champion, when he played there in the Carolina League. The one hit by George that March afternoon went 60 feet farther.

To add icing to the cake, George came on to pitch the last two innings, shutting down a Sparrows comeback and securing a 15–9 win for the Buzzards.

Rodger Pippen, who played center field for the Orioles and later became George's roommate on the road, also doubled as a freelance sportswriter, and he was sending daily reports on the team's spring training to the newspaper back in Baltimore. In the story he sent back that night, Pippen described the situation of the game in the second inning and wrote: "The next batter made a hit that will live in the memory of all who saw it. That clouter was George Ruth, the southpaw from St. Mary's school. The ball carried so far to right field that he walked around the bases."

Both newspapers back home carried stories about the game the next day, and the headlines on both were about George's home run. "Homer by Ruth Feature of Game," the *Baltimore Sun* said. "Ruth Makes Mighty Clout," the *Baltimore American* echoed. George Ruth wasn't often out of the headlines on sports pages for the rest of his career.

It wasn't long after arriving in Fayetteville, that young Ruth ceased to be known as George, either to fans or sportswriters. The story of how he got the name Babe has almost as many versions as the one about his childhood. Some said he was teased because of his baby face, and that was shortened to Babe. Others said that because of his youth, inexperience, and gullibility, the veteran players called him a babe in the woods, and the name stuck. Someone must have called George "a babe in the woods," because he repeats that story himself in his autobiography. But the way the name really came about is less intriguing.

Every spring Jack Dunn would bring three or four

new prospects to training camp. These were always young players he had found during his scouting for talent among the sandlots and schools around the Baltimore area. Usually they didn't work out very well, but for a while they were Dunn's pet players, and they were always referred to by the regulars as "Dunn's babes."

Soon after training camp opened, one of the veterans who had noticed young Ruth asked a teammate who he was. The teammate shrugged and replied, "He's one of Dunnie's babes." After he followed his home run with other exploits, as both a pitcher and hitter, the older players were still calling him "Babe," but this time it was out of respect rather than as a joke. By the third week of spring training, even the Baltimore papers were referring to him in stories as Babe Ruth, rather than George. Then the fans were cheering for Babe, and before long more people knew the name Babe Ruth than that of the president.

As spring training wore on, the older players slowly came to accept Ruth as a member of the team. There was quite simply no way to deny his ability as both a hitter and a pitcher. But there is a wide difference between being accepted and being embraced, and George remained mostly an outsider to the veterans on the Orioles team throughout the team's time in Fayetteville.

The truth is that George had little in common with the players. He had traveled from what was essentially a reform-school environment with its strict supervision to a freedom he had never experienced before. He made friends more easily with the younger boys who hung around the ballpark to watch the Orioles than with the other players on the team.

One of those boys had a bicycle, and George asked if he could borrow it. One of George's childhood dreams had been to own a bicycle, but his parents never had the money to buy him one, and there were no bicycles at St. Mary's. In fact, George had never even ridden one, and as he was trying to learn by riding it around the streets near the ballpark, he turned a corner and nearly ran over Dunn. George swerved and rode into a truck, fell over, and looked up at Dunn sheepishly with the bike lying on top of him. Dunn growled, "If you want to go back to the Home, kid, just keep riding those bicycles."

On the other hand, Dunn was ecstatic about George's progress on the field. When it came time to announce who would be on the team that he would take back north with him for the regular International League season, Ruth was on the roster. In an interview, Dunn was glowing in his praise for the player now known as the Babe.

"He has all the earmarks of a great ballplayer," Dunn said of young Ruth. "He hits like a fiend and he seems to be at home in any position, even though he's left-handed. He's the most promising young ballplayer I've ever had."

Professional baseball in those days was structured pretty much the same as it is today. There were the major leagues, divided into the older National League and the younger American League. Some major American cities—like New York, Boston, Chicago, Philadelphia, and St. Louis—had two major-league teams, one in each league. Teams in other cities played in the minor leagues, which there were several of. The Orioles, for example, played in the International League, one of the top minor leagues.

The minor-league teams were for the most part

owned outright by individuals such as Dunn, who owned the Baltimore Orioles. There was no extensive farm system as there is today in which a major-league franchise may own and operate several minor-league clubs, although the Boston Red Sox owner bought the Providence, Rhode Island, minor-league team the year Ruth started playing.

It was also the custom in those days, even for minor-league teams, to play a series of exhibition games before the start of the regular season. Often the minor-league teams would play a major-league team. It gave the managers a chance to see some of their new talent play against the best teams in the game, and it also brought in some money to help defray the costs of spring training.

Dunn played Ruth in two games against the Philadelphia Phillies, who had finished second in the National League the previous year. Babe pitched three innings in each game, and the Orioles won both of them. Ruth had been solid if not spectacular. The Orioles then traveled up to Wilmington, Delaware, to play the Philadelphia Athletics, which in 1914 was the best team in baseball. They had won three

American League titles and three World Series in the past four years, and were managed by baseball legend Connie Mack.

Dunn wanted to show off his new star, and Ruth did not disappoint him. Although he gave up a total of 13 hits, Babe pitched a complete nine-inning game and allowed only two runs as the Orioles beat the world champions 6–2. Dunn was so elated, he scheduled another game with the Athletics for the Orioles exhibition opener when the team finally returned to Baltimore the following week.

When they arrived back home, George was surprised to find that his picture was in all the newspapers and that his new name—Babe Ruth—was immortalized in print. Dunn, who was nothing if not a showman, had persuaded the sportswriters to promote the upcoming rematch with the Philadelphia Athletics, even though it was still exhibition season. It worked, and a huge crowd came out to see the game, although probably as many of the fans were on hand to see the A's as to see the new kid Ruth.

Whether it was hometown jitters or just an off day, Babe didn't exactly live up to his advance billing in his first game as a pro in Baltimore. He gave up three straight doubles in the first inning, and four runs in the four innings he pitched. The A's easily won the game 12–5.

But one of the beauties of baseball is that if you play terribly one day, you can get a chance at redemption the next. There was still a week of exhibition games left before the regular season started, and Dunn played Ruth in a game against the Brooklyn Dodgers. It was in that game that Ruth showed a glimpse of the player he would become.

Dunn started him as pitcher, and the Babe had his good stuff plus control. He held the Dodgers hitless through the first several innings, and when he came up to bat for the first time, he hit a long drive deep into right field that the Dodgers' young star Casey Stengel managed to catch after a long run. The next time Ruth came up, Stengel moved farther back in the outfield. But Ruth whacked such a hit that Stengel, running with all his might, couldn't catch up to it. It went over his head, and the Babe wound up on third base with a triple. Years later, Stengel reminisced about that game:

We had never heard of him. He had good stuff, a good fastball, a fine curve—a dipsy-do that made you think a little. When he hit that long fly I was embarrassed. Me, a big leaguer, underplaying him. But no one had ever heard of him—especially as a batter. We lost the game. The kid beats us pitching and he beats us batting.

By the time the International League season opened, Ruth was a fixture with the Orioles. The two other rookies from spring training, including Morrisette, ended up being cut. George was the only one of Dunn's babes that year to make the team, and Dunn doubled his salary, from the $600 he had been promised to $1,200. When he got his first paycheck, Babe went out and bought himself a bicycle.

Ruth pitched the second game of the regular season for the Orioles. He was somewhat less than awesome in the first inning. He walked a batter, threw a wild pitch, and hit yet another batter. He had the bases loaded with one out, but he managed to get out of the inning. By the second inning, he had calmed down, and he ended up pitching a 6–0 shutout, contributing to his own victory with two hits in four times at bat.

In another game that first week, Ruth went into a tie game in the tenth inning as a relief pitcher and held the opposing team hitless. In the eleventh he hit a towering fly that went over the left fielder's head and scored the winning run from first base. Throughout that first month, at home in Baltimore or on his first road trip, Ruth was up and down. But he was mostly up. He would win one game, then lose one, then win two more. In one game in Providence, he was pulled for a reliever in the second inning. And in Jersey City, he blew a five-run lead in the eighth. In Newark, however, he pitched back-to-back games in a doubleheader and got both wins. He had an 8–1 lead in the opener, but then got wild and was relieved. But the Orioles hung on and won. Then he came right back to pitch the second game and threw a complete 11-inning shutout, which the Orioles won 1–0.

His hitting was also inconsistent. During the first couple of weeks, he had a batting average of over .300, but he then went into a slump and his average fell to .200. But in city after city, team after team began to realize that when Ruth came up to the plate, the outfielders had to move back. Because if he connected, he could hit the ball farther than anybody else.

In June, the Orioles got hot and went on a 13-game winning streak. By early July, they had a 47–22 won-lost record and were leading the International League by five games. Ruth pitched the opening game of a big July 4 doubleheader and won it 4–1. Despite his ups and downs during the first half of the season, Ruth had a 14–6 won-lost record as a pitcher, and his hitting was becoming more consistent.

Two days later, the Babe came on in relief with the bases loaded and nobody out, and retired the next three batters to preserve a win. It was the last time he pitched for Baltimore.

FOUR

IF BASEBALL HAS always been the national pastime, it also has always been a business. And as much as Jack Dunn was a fan of the game and a judge of baseball talent, he was also a keen businessman. Dunn could put together the greatest team in organized baseball, but if nobody came to watch them, then he was just paying nine talented guys to go out and play.

Dunn was not a stingy man. He had raised Ruth's salary at the start of the season, and at the beginning of June he raised it again, another $600. What started as a $600 contract for the season was now $1,800, and Dunn still figured he was getting a bargain. Part of the reason Dunn kept raising Ruth's salary was that he had a new rival for the Baltimore fans' allegiance. He was afraid the rival would offer Ruth more, and he would take it.

The biggest headache Dunn had that summer of 1914 was not how his team was playing but the fact that nobody in Baltimore was coming to watch the Orioles. The previous year, a group of wealthy men around the East Coast had organized a new operation called the Federal League, which they intended to be a third major league in baseball. Both the National League and the newer American League regarded the Federal League as an outlaw operation and refused to recognize it.

There was enough money behind the Federals, however, that it awarded franchises to several cities, and Baltimore was one of them. At one time, Baltimore had been a major-league city, and it would be again, but that original franchise had moved away, and for a number of years, Dunn's minor-league Orioles had been the only game in town. But when the Federal League came along, Baltimore fans switched their loyalty to the new local franchise, called the Terrapins, and there were a lot of empty seats for the Orioles' games.

For example, when Ruth played his first regular season game as an Oriole—pitching a six-hit shutout and going two for four at the plate—fewer than two hundred fans were in the stadium to see it. It was the smallest crowd yet to see the Orioles play. Across the street, the Terrapins of the Federal League had over two thousand people in the stands.

At the time, baseball players pretty much had the status of slaves to the club owners. There was no free agency and no collective bargaining. When a ballplayer signed a contract with a team owner, he played for that team. He couldn't test the market to see if he could get more money from another team. There was an informal agreement among the baseball owners that one team would not poach players from another team. An owner might sell a player's contract to another team, but the player had no say in such a deal. The only leverage a player had, even when his contract expired, was to refuse to play.

The new Federal League, however, was not bound by the rules by which the other major-league teams operated. The new franchises in this so-called third major league were offering contracts to disgruntled players for more money than they were making in the other leagues. There were rumors that the established major-league teams would ban players who left for the Federal League from ever playing in the American or National Leagues again. But it did not stop many players from accepting offers to play in the Federal League.

Dunn's biggest fear was that the Federal League would steal Ruth. There had been rumors that the Terrapins had already offered Ruth a $10,000 bonus and a salary of $10,000 if he would come play across the street. They were denied at the time, but Ruth said in *The Babe Ruth Story* that such an offer had been made, but he turned it down. Not only did he feel a certain loyalty to Dunn, but he also was afraid he might be barred from ever playing in the major leagues if he accepted it. Also, he was still officially under the guardianship of St. Mary's, and any new contract would require Brother Paul's approval.

One incident illustrates the extent of Dunn's worries about his newest Babe. When the Orioles were in Baltimore, Ruth hung his hat and slept at his father's apartment above the saloon, but he rarely spent any time there. He visited St. Mary's often when he was in town and felt more at home with the kids there than with his teammates. One day early in the season, Ruth came to Dunn and asked for six passes for that day's game. Dunn was suspicious. Was Ruth inviting Federal League scouts?

"Who are they for?" Dunn asked.

"Friends of mine," Ruth replied.

Dunn gave him six passes but kept watching to see who would show up to claim them. When Ruth arrived at the ballpark, he had six youngsters from St. Mary's trailing behind him. Dunn walked up to greet them.

"These your friends?" he asked Babe.

Ruth nodded and led the boys to their seats.

But even if the Terrapins did not steal Ruth, the novelty of the Federal League was still stealing fans and the city's affection from Dunn's team. The Baltimore newspapers still covered the Orioles, but the big headlines were for the Terrapins. The new league was still a novelty, and Baltimore fans wanted to see what was billed as major-league baseball rather than the minor-league team they knew. Attendance didn't improve as the season wore on, even when the Orioles got hot in June and won 13 straight games. At one point, the Orioles played before only 150 people. Dunn was losing money, and he had to do something or he would soon be broke.

One of his options was to move the team to another city. He negotiated with some men in Richmond, Virginia, but he was reluctant to leave Baltimore. There was some high-level talk about forming an officially sanctioned third major league—one to rival the Federal League—with Dunn getting one of the franchises for Baltimore. But the National and American League owners couldn't agree on a plan, and it fizzled. By the beginning of July, Dunn decided he had to sell off some of his players to avoid bankruptcy.

The Orioles had such a good team that several major-league clubs were interested in buying some of its players. Dunn went on a selling spree, and in three days in early July, he sold four of his starting lineup and two of his starting pitchers. The three deals brought him nearly $50,000 and kept the franchise solvent. But without those star players, the Orioles began to nose-dive in the standings and finished near the cellar.

By far the biggest transaction involved selling

three players to the Boston Red Sox—Ben Egan, the Orioles catcher and captain; Ernie Shore, a pitching prospect who had just graduated from college; and Babe Ruth, the kid from reform school who could be either brilliant or erratic on any given day. It was reported that Dunn got between $25,000 and $30,000 for the three players.

The Red Sox had a new owner, Joseph J. Lannin, who had bought the team the previous year and named Bill Carrigan as manager. The two men shared the opinion that nothing is more important to the success of a baseball team than good pitching.

As soon as the new players arrived at Boston's Back Bay station, they walked to Landers coffee shop for breakfast. Ruth was feeling on top of the world. He was a major-league baseball player only four months after leaving St. Mary's school, and the $1,800 he was making was more money than he ever dreamed existed. He ordered a plate of eggs and bacon and began flirting with the waitress, a pretty girl named Helen Woodford. In the days and weeks to come, Babe would eat breakfast every morning at Landers, and he began dating Helen, who was sixteen years old and the first real girlfriend he had ever had.

It would be great to report that Babe Ruth took the major leagues by storm from the moment he arrived in Boston. But his first season with the Red Sox was full of ups and downs. Carrigan started Ruth as pitcher in a game against the Cleveland Indians on the day he arrived, only hours after he stepped off the train. The Red Sox were far down in the standings, and one of the reasons Lannin had bought Ruth and Shore was in the hopes that their young arms could lift the team into contention in the pennant race.

In the very first inning of his major-league career, Ruth made a play that showed his natural baseball instincts. He gave up a single to the leadoff hitter, who then went to second on a groundout. The next batter was Shoeless Joe Jackson, and he hit a single to Tris Speaker in center field. When Speaker threw toward home, the runner trying to score from second held up at third base. Ruth quickly cut off the throw and whipped the ball to first to hold Jackson to a single. The runner on third then broke for home, but the first baseman threw him out at the plate. As a result of Ruth's play, the Indians had a runner at first base and two outs instead of one out and runners at second and third. Ruth then picked off Jackson at first to end the inning.

Ruth stayed in the game into the seventh inning, when Carrigan sent a pinch hitter in for him. It was one of the few times in his career that somebody pinch-hit for Babe Ruth. Still, the Red Sox hung on to win, and Ruth had his first major-league victory. A few days later, Carrigan again pitched Ruth, this time against the Detroit Tigers. But he was erratic and he went only three innings before the manager pulled him. From then on, for the next month, Ruth sat on the bench. He didn't pitch a single inning and he was never called on to pinch-hit. In the middle of August, the Red Sox decided to send Ruth down to the minors, to the Providence Grays in the International League, the team Lannin had just bought.

There was never a convincing reason given for the decision except that the Providence team was making a run at the International League championship, and they thought Ruth could help their new farm club. Ruth was unhappy about it. For one thing, it separated him from Helen, whom he was now seeing every day. Also, he was worried that his major-league career might be over before it had even begun.

Oddly enough, it was about this time Ruth received his first fan letter—in fact, the only fan letter he got that first season. It was from Brother Matthias, and it said: "You're doing fine, George. I'm proud of you." It was as though Brother Matthias knew exactly

After being sold by Baltimore to Boston in 1914,
Babe was sent down to their farm team in Providence.

when George might need some encouragement. Ruth kept the letter for the rest of his life.

The Providence Grays, or Clamdiggers as they were unofficially known, were managed by Wild Bill Donovan, and he started using Ruth as often as he could as soon as he arrived. In his first game, Ruth pitched and hit two triples to lead the Grays to a win over Rochester and move his team into first place.

Through the rest of August and into September, the Grays were locked in a pennant race against Rochester, New York, and Donovan was pitching Ruth and his other star, Carl Mays, almost every other day. Pitchers usually had three days' rest between starts in those years, but it was not uncommon for them to pitch more often.

As the season drew to a finale, Ruth pitched and won four games over the space of eight days. Mays did no less, once pitching both games of a doubleheader. Then Ruth pitched the first game of a doubleheader the following day, and came back in relief in the second game. Ruth was also swinging well and was hitting over .300 during the Grays' run for the title. Donovan's strategy and the heroics of Ruth paid off.

By the final weekend of the season, Providence had clinched the International League title.

In the last game of the Grays' season, Ruth played right field against his old club, the Baltimore Orioles. He had three hits, stole two bases, scored three runs, and made a diving catch in the outfield.

After Providence won the championship, the American League still had a week or more to go in its season, and the Red Sox recalled him to the team. By this time, the Red Sox were out of the American League pennant race, but they were solidly in second place, a marked improvement over the previous year. The local heroes that year were the Boston Braves, the National League team across town. The Braves, a franchise that would eventually move to Milwaukee and later Atlanta, ended up winning, against all odds, the World Series that year and were the toast of the town as the "Miracle Braves."

Ruth was given one more start in that last week with the Red Sox. He pitched against the New York Yankees and won the game 11–5. He had his first major-league hit in that game, a double, and he ended up scoring his first major-league run.

Despite his being benched for nearly a month, it was a remarkable rookie year. From the playground at St. Mary's, Ruth had played for three teams, in Baltimore, Boston, and Providence. His overall record as a pitcher, counting some exhibition games, was 28 wins and 9 losses. If his overall batting average was not so spectacular (he hit .300 in the International League and .200 for Boston), he had showed he could hit the long ball. Nearly half of his hits were for extra bases, including nine triples and one home run.

With the season over, Babe was planning to return to Baltimore for the winter, but he was torn over the prospect of not seeing Helen again until the following spring. His solution to this problem says more about his impetuosity than anything else.

As he was sitting in Landers coffee shop one morning, he looked up from his plate of eggs and bacon and said, "Hon, how about you and me getting married?"

Helen, who had just turned seventeen, said yes. They had known each other less than three months, and the Babe had been out of town on road trips through much of that time. However, two days later, Helen quit her job, and she and Ruth traveled to

Baltimore together. They stayed with Babe's father, who had since remarried. Two days after Babe and Helen arrived, they went to apply for a marriage license. Because he was not yet the legal age of twenty-one, or thought he wasn't, Ruth got his dad to write a letter of consent for him to get married. Helen, who came from an extended family in South Boston—she had four brothers and three sisters—simply lied about her age, saying she was eighteen. Her mother and father certainly had no objection to one of their daughters getting married.

They were wed on October 17 in St. Paul's Catholic Church in Ellicott City, a little town west of Baltimore. It was a small, private wedding, and they celebrated at a party in the saloon Babe's dad ran at the time on Conway Street. There was no report of a honeymoon trip, and the newlyweds spent the winter in one of two apartments above the bar where Ruth's dad and stepmother lived. If Babe and his dad were never exactly chums, they had reached a point in their relationship where they could get along. There certainly was no question now of Big George taking a horsewhip to Little George.

FIVE

IN MARCH, BABE left Helen with his dad and stepmother in Baltimore and reported to training camp. He took the train back to Boston, and then another one with the team to Hot Springs, Arkansas. The Babe Ruth who arrived at spring training that year was a very different young man from the George Ruth who showed up in North Carolina a year earlier.

For one thing, he had turned twenty-one—or thought he had—and was no longer under anyone's guardianship. He was legally an adult. He was married and earning more money in a summer of playing ball than most people earned in a year. His picture had been in newspapers and his name in headlines. He had traveled to all the major cities in the eastern half of the country, and to Canada, and he went first class.

He was savvy. No one would ever get him to ride a sleeper train with his arm in the clothes hammock again.

Throughout spring training the Red Sox played only intramural games. Carrigan was counting on pitching more than hitting for the Red Sox to win the pennant, and he didn't want to tire out his lineup of pitchers. It was a theory that nearly backfired on him.

By the time the season opened in April, the Red Sox had played only one exhibition game against another major-league team. And Ruth, in fact, was not even considered one of the top four pitchers. While Carrigan thought the Babe had a lot of promise, his occasional bouts of wildness kept him out of Carrigan's starting rotation.

The Red Sox season started terribly. The lack of play during spring training soon took its toll on the team. The hitting was rusty and the pitching erratic, and within a week, two of the starting pitchers were sidelined with injuries. Carrigan turned to Ruth.

He had come on in one game as a relief pitcher and done well, so Carrigan put him in to start a game. Ruth won 9–2. Carrigan started him again a few days

Babe was primarily known as a pitching ace with the Red Sox. He is shown here warming up before a game in 1915.

later, this time against the New York Yankees, and it proved to be a turning point, although Ruth lost the game 3–2 in extra innings. For one thing, he pitched solidly for 13 innings. For another, he hit a home run.

The Yankees in those days played their home

games at the Polo Grounds, which was the stadium of the National League's New York Giants, on the far Upper East Side of Manhattan. In the third inning, the Babe hit a towering home run into the upper-right-field stands. Carrigan realized that day that while the Babe could be effective as a pitcher, he was a natural hitter. Carrigan kept him on the mound, but from then on he was a regular starter. And the manager occasionally used him as a pinch hitter, a rarity for a pitcher.

The Red Sox, who had great expectations for winning the pennant that year, bumbled along through the first half of the season. By June, they were far down in the standings. Then the team caught fire and went on a winning streak with the Babe at the center of it. Ruth, who at the start of the summer was 1–4 as a pitcher, found his control both from the mound and at the plate. He hit another home run at the Polo Grounds against the Yankees that was even longer than the first, and the fans in New York were beginning to take notice. One sportswriter wrote after the second homer: "His name is Babe Ruth. He is built like a bale of cotton and pitches left-handed for the

Boston Red Sox. All left-handers are peculiar and Babe is no exception, because he can also bat."

In the second half of the season, Ruth won 17 of 21 games he pitched, and ended the year with an 18–8 record. He also was the second-best hitter on the team.

Tris Speaker was still the star of the 1915 Red Sox team. The center fielder was the best fielder, the best base runner, and the best hitter, batting .322 for the season. The only other hitter to bat over .300 was Ruth, who posted a .315 average in the games that he played. Speaker, of course, played nearly every day, while Ruth got to the plate only in games he pitched and a few times as a pinch hitter. But between Speaker and Ruth, it was the Babe who was the slugger. Of Ruth's 29 hits that season, 15 were for extra bases and 4 were home runs, twice as many homers as any other player on the team.

Another big favorite of the Red Sox fans was Duffy Lewis, the left fielder. Before the Green Monster wall was built, left field at Fenway Park—the Red Sox home field—ended in a steep embankment. Lewis used to race up it like a mountain goat to snag fly balls hit there by opposing batters, and the big mound became known as Duffy's Cliff.

The Red Sox won the pennant that year and played the Philadelphia Phillies in the World Series. For reasons only Carrigan knew, the manager did not start Ruth in any of the games. Boston won the Series four games to one, but Ruth stayed on the bench for all five games except for one pinch hit, in which he grounded out to first. If the Babe was disappointed at not getting a World Series start, his check for being part of the World Championship team helped offset it. His part of the winners' share was more than his annual salary.

Ruth and Helen had been living in a rented apartment in Cambridge during the season, but they didn't want to spend the winter there. They had little to do with Helen's parents, so they returned to Baltimore. Babe used part of his World Series bonus to buy his father a new tavern on the corner of Lombard and Eutaw streets, and sometimes Babe even worked there behind the bar.

The following spring, as he was preparing to return to Arkansas for training camp, some surprises were in store. For one thing, the Federal League had gone out of business. The novelty value of a rival enterprise challenging the two established leagues of Major League Baseball had worn off, and attendance began to drop. As a result, the high salaries that teams in the American and National Leagues had been paying their players to keep them from jumping to the Federals suddenly evaporated. Many players, even stars, who had received big pay raises the preceding three years now faced pay cuts.

Though it was a fortune to a kid who grew up in a reform school, Ruth's salary was not so astronomical that he was affected. Also, he still had a year to go on the contract he had signed in 1914. However, Joe Lannin decided to save money on some of his other players. Tris Speaker's contract was up, and Lannin offered him a new one at a 40 percent reduction in pay—from $15,000 a year to $9,000 a year. Speaker refused to sign.

The great center fielder showed up at spring training without a contract, and everyone in baseball, including the other Red Sox players and their manager, Carrigan, assumed a deal would be worked out before the season started. But both Lannin and Speaker remained firm, and two days before the opening game, Lannin announced that he had sold Speaker to the Cleveland Indians, a mediocre team in the second division.

No one was more surprised than Carrigan. The manager and owner had enjoyed a good relationship until then, consulting on almost all issues, whether on the field or off. But Lannin had made this sale without even telling Carrigan. The rest of the team was downcast at losing their star player, and Carrigan tried to rally them with a pep talk. He called the team together and told them:

> All right, we've lost Speaker. That means we're not going to score as many runs. But we're still a good team. We have the pitching. We have the fielding. And we'll hit well enough. We'll win the pennant again if you guys stop your moaning and get down to business.

The Red Sox started great. Ruth pitched on opening day and won, 2–1. And the club won six of its first eight games. But they missed Speaker and the offensive spark he created. The losses, many of them one- or two-run decisions, started to accumulate, and they dropped far behind in the standings.

Ruth tried to fill the void left by Speaker almost single-handedly. He started off winning his first four games and was having his best year as a pitcher so far in his career. He was also hitting consistently. At one point in the summer he hit home runs in three successive games, and his batting average again climbed over .300. Carrigan even talked about moving Ruth to the outfield so he could have his bat at the plate every day, but since Babe was also his best pitcher, he didn't want to take him off the mound.

By the middle of August, the Red Sox were back in the thick of things. Babe pitched three winning games over a space of seven days, and Boston went on a winning streak that put them in the American League lead. Then, with only two weeks left to play, Lannin dropped another bombshell. He announced that Carrigan would retire as manager at the end of that season. It was Carrigan's decision, but the announcement caught the entire team by surprise, and the Red Sox went into a nosedive that knocked them from first place in the standings into third, behind Chicago and Detroit.

But as another great player and manager, Yogi Berra, would say decades later, in baseball "it ain't over till it's over." The Red Sox pulled themselves out of the doldrums during the final week and won five straight games against their two rivals.

In Chicago, Ruth pitched the first of a two-game series before forty thousand fans, at that time the largest crowd ever to see a baseball game in the Windy City. He won it 6–2 for his twentieth victory of the season. Then the Red Sox won the next day as well, while Detroit was losing to the Philadelphia Athletics, then the lowliest team in baseball. That set up a three-game showdown with Detroit, starting the following day.

Boston swept all three games against the Tigers, with Ruth winning the finale by a score of 10–2. The Red Sox had once again won the American League pennant and would face the Brooklyn Dodgers in the World Series. It had been a stellar year for Ruth, who ended up with 23 wins as pitcher, including nine complete shutouts.

This time, Carrigan did not hesitate to use Ruth in the World Series and started him in the second game against Brooklyn at Fenway Park. In the first inning, Hy Myers hit a long drive to right-center field. It was a ball that Tris Speaker could probably have caught, but it got past both the Boston center fielder and right fielder, and Myers ended up scoring an inside-the-park home run. Brooklyn had a 1–0 lead. In the third inning, Ruth knocked in a run that evened the score. The game remained tied 1–1 into the fourteenth inning, and Ruth was still pitching when Boston won it 2–1. The Red Sox went on to beat the Dodgers four games to one for their second World Series title in a row.

Immediately after the Series ended, the Babe and Helen went on a hunting trip to New Hampshire with some of the other players and their wives. It was their first real vacation together, and they had a great time.

During the course of that season, Ruth and Helen took a lease on an eighty-acre farm near Sudbury, about twenty miles west of Boston. It was an arrangement that worked well at the start, especially since the Babe was gone about half the time on road trips with the ball club. But after a while, Helen began to feel lonely, especially when her husband began to stay in town in Boston after games he pitched. Helen also began to hear rumors that Babe was seeing other women, especially when he was on the road, but also some of the nights he stayed over in town.

Ruth's philandering became so open that it would have been impossible for Helen not to know. Once during the season, when the Red Sox were playing in Washington, Babe asked Carrigan permission to go to Baltimore to visit his father on a day when there was no game. Carrigan, glad to see the Babe doing his family duty, agreed. The problem came when his dad showed up at the ballpark for the next day's game and had a seat near the Red Sox dugout.

"You're a fine son, George," Ruth senior shouted at Babe. "Down in this neighborhood and don't even come by to see your father." Carrigan just stared at Ruth, who said nothing.

In the late fall, Ruth got word of another shock from the Red Sox. After losing Tris Speaker at the start of the previous year and Carrigan after the season ended, Lannin announced in November that he was selling the team to Harry Frazee, a New York theatrical producer whose only venture in sports had been to stage a championship boxing match between Jack Johnson and Jess Willard in Havana, Cuba, the year before.

Frazee's purchase of the Red Sox ended up being the death knell for them as a premier team in baseball for years to come, although at the time he made few changes, except to bring in Jack Barry as his manager. One other change he made was to allow the wives of players to join the team for spring training in Hot Springs, and Helen went to Arkansas with Babe the following March.

It was a lighter atmosphere in the camp with the wives present. Helen learned to ride horseback, and one day when Babe was warming up she sat on her horse and watched him. Babe was throwing to Joe Devine, the new Red Sox catcher, but he kept watching Helen. He would wind up and hurl the ball to Devine without even looking at him, keeping his eyes on Helen on the horse. "I'm working on my control," he joked.

Babe, Helen, and some of the players often went bowling, and Ruth was so good at it the others made him bowl with his right hand as a handicap. He tried joining a barbershop quartet that some of the players formed, but his high-pitched voice was so out of tune the others jokingly told him to come back after his voice changed. He loved to play poker with the other guys, but he was so bad at it that Devine told him he should just leave some money on the table and go to the movies.

Back in Boston, the 1917 season started out well. Babe, now twenty-two but thinking he was twenty-three, pitched on opening day and won a 10–0 shutout. He won his first eight games, and by June his record was 10–1, and the Red Sox were again in first place. But events that had been preoccupying the rest of the world caught up with major-league baseball.

In April of that year, the United States finally decided to enter World War I on the side of England, France, and Italy against Germany, and a military draft of young men for the army would inevitably deplete the teams. Babe, as a married man, was exempt from the draft, but so many other players were in line to go into uniform that there was even talk of suspending the rest of the season.

Whether it was because of the war or the personal problems that were beginning to surface in his marriage, Babe grew increasingly combative through the summer, both on the field and off. His temper reached a peak in a game in Boston on June 23. The first batter up in the first inning was given a walk by umpire Brick Owens on four straight pitches. Ruth complained and shouted invectives at the umpire after each pitch, and when Owens shouted "ball four," Ruth ran toward home plate.

Owens told him to get back to the mound and pitch or he would throw him out of the game. Ruth countered that if he ejected him, "I'll bust you one on the nose." The ump immediately thumbed him out of the game. The Babe charged at him. The Boston catcher tried to stop him, but Ruth swung over his shoulder and hit the umpire on the shoulder.

The game is further notable because Ernie Shore, who was brought in to pitch for the ejected Ruth, made history. The runner Ruth walked was thrown out trying to steal on Shore's first pitch. Shore then retired the next 26 batters in a row for a perfect no-hit, no-run game. At the time it was regarded as only the fourth perfect game pitched in baseball history, but it is remembered mainly because of Ruth's ejection.

Whether the game was actually a perfect game was long disputed by baseball buffs, since Shore didn't face all 27 batters. In 1991, major-league baseball appointed a Committee for Statistical Accuracy to examine all of the records in the history of the game. The ruling on that particular game was that it was "a combined no-hitter" between Shore and George Herman Ruth.

As for Ruth's swing at the ump, he was suspended indefinitely, although it ended up being for only ten days. After his return, Babe was erratic. He lost his first two games after the suspension, and the Red Sox began to unravel. By September, the Red Sox were out of the pennant race, and several of their players—including Jack Barry, the playing manager, and Shore—had been drafted or had joined the navy. Ruth ended up winning 24 games in a season that had otherwise been a disappointment.

Another disappointment at the end of that season was in his personal life. Things were not happy between Babe and Helen, a situation brought on mainly by Babe's wandering eye. Until now, most of his philandering had come when he was on the road with the team. But his escapades with women were getting closer to home. One night in October, he was driving one of his cars when he had a serious accident with a Boston trolley car. Babe was not hurt, but a young woman in the car with him was injured badly enough to be hospitalized. The young woman was not Helen. The story made the newspapers, and Helen could no longer pretend not to notice Babe's extra-marital affairs. They quarreled, and Babe promised to reform.

As the 1918 season got under way, the loss of so many players to the draft took its toll on baseball. With Jack Barry now in the military, for example, Frazee had to find a new manager for the Red Sox. He hired Ed Barrow, who had been president of the International League. Barrow, who had no experience as a manager, then hired Harry Hooper to be what today would be called a bench coach to help him out. The 1918 season was Ruth's last as a starting pitcher, and one of the reasons was that the Babe was hitting like the slugger he always was.

Throughout spring training and the exhibition season, Babe had been blistering the ball, hitting home runs in several games. Sportswriters began writing more about his hitting than his pitching, and the fans started coming out on days he was scheduled to pitch just to watch him hit. Babe again pitched the 1918 season opener and won it. In his fifth start of the year, against the Yankees, he hit a home run that went over the stands in right field at the Polo Grounds. The fans went wild.

Hooper told Barrow he should start using Ruth in left field on the days he didn't pitch so the Red Sox could have the daily benefit of his hitting. But Barrow resisted. "I'd be the laughingstock of baseball if I changed the best left-hander in the game into an outfielder," he told Hooper.

When Boston's first baseman slightly injured his hand, Barrow relented and put Ruth in the lineup at first base, batting sixth. It was the first time Ruth had started a major-league game in any position other than pitcher, and the first time he had batted anywhere in the lineup except ninth. He hit another home run.

Barrow put Ruth back at first base the next day and moved him into cleanup position in the batting order. He hit another home run. Two days later, it was his turn to pitch, and he had five hits—a single, three doubles, and a triple. By the middle of May, Babe was hitting .484, and the fans cheered him every time he walked to the plate.

Then in late May, what started as a bad cold and sore throat almost ended his career. On an off day, Babe and Helen went on a picnic to the beach. It was raw and cold, and his temperature climbed to 104 degrees. He thought it was the flu, and when he showed up the next day at the ballpark, the Red Sox trainer treated his throat with silver nitrate, a common practice in those days. However, the trainer used too much, and Ruth's throat swelled to the point where he had trouble breathing. He was rushed to a hospital, where an antidote was given. He stayed there a week. One lasting effect of the episode was that for the rest of his life, Babe's naturally high-pitched voice had a raspy tone.

When Babe returned to the club at the end of the month, he announced to Barrow that he didn't want to pitch anymore, that he wanted to play every day and concentrate on his hitting. After all, that was what the fans liked to see him do most.

Barrow was furious and ordered Ruth to pitch his next start. The Babe said he couldn't, that his left wrist was hurt. The feud reached an impasse in Washington when an argument over Ruth swinging at a first pitch ended with a threat by Ruth to punch Barrow on the nose. Barrow fined Ruth five hundred dollars, and Babe stalked out, saying, "I quit."

The Babe left town and went to visit his father. He even contacted a team at the Chester Shipyards in Pennsylvania about playing for them. With the help of intermediaries, Ruth and Barrow settled their differences, though some residual rancor remained and would have ramifications on the Babe's career in years to come.

For the rest of the season, Ruth did it all. He pitched, and played left field and first base. The Red Sox were in a pennant race, and it was Babe's arm and bat that eventually won it. In a doubleheader in Cleveland, he pitched the opener, then played left field in the second game. In another game, he pitched against the St. Louis Browns and hit fourth in the lineup—one of the few times in baseball that the pitcher batted cleanup.

In the home stretch of the season, Ruth won seven games as a pitcher and led the Red Sox in hitting. Overall, he had a 13–7 record on the mound, but won 9 of his last 11 starts. He had played 59 games in the outfield and 13 at first base, and had hit an even .300 on the year. More than half his hits had been for extra bases. Although the home runs dropped off, he ended up with 11, tied for first place.

Because of the war, there had been talk of halting the baseball season in August. It did not seem right to some that grown men were playing baseball at a time when American boys were dying on the battlefields of Europe. In the end, it was decided to curtail the season, ending it on Labor Day.

During the last week of the season, however, Babe got word that his father had died. Ruth senior had been trying to stop a domestic dispute that erupted in his bar in Baltimore. He became embroiled in the fight and fell, hitting the back of his head. He died that night in a hospital. Babe and Helen went to Baltimore for the funeral, and he missed three games.

The Red Sox won the 1918 World Series four games to two over the Chicago Cubs. Ruth got two of the wins, and in the course of the series completed 29 innings of scoreless pitching in World Series play, dating back to the previous year. It broke the record of 28 that had been set by Christy Mathewson in 1905. Babe's record would stand for forty-two years, and he would later say he was more proud of that record than all his home-run marks.

That championship, however, was the last World Series the Red Sox would win for eighty-six years.

SIX

DURING THE WAR frenzy that cut short the 1918 season, there had been talk of canceling the 1919 baseball season altogether. Two months after the 1918 World Series, however, the war ended. But the little baseball skirmishes that had broken out in the Red Sox clubhouse and dugout in 1918 continued to fester throughout the winter, and by the time spring training rolled around, the air was ripe for a renewal of full-scale hostilities.

It started when Ruth informed the Red Sox that he wanted a sizable increase in salary for the new season. Babe had become aware that many fans came out to the ballpark as much to see him play as to root for the home team. He was also taking on the aura of celebrity in an age where the status of celebrity was usually reserved for movie stars. A cigar had already been named for him, and he was always looking for ways to get other endorsements. Ruth constantly needed more money to support his lifestyle. He spent it almost as fast as he earned it—on cars, on silk suits and shirts, on the horses, on the girls he saw on the side, and, not least, on Helen.

The strains in his marriage were becoming tighter. Although she and Babe had been married for four years, Helen was still only twenty-one years old, and she was growing tired of being left on the farm in Sudbury while Babe stayed in town partying or hanging out with his cronies. The only way Babe knew to try to make amends was to buy Helen expensive gifts, which he did more and more frequently.

Babe's spending habits included more than luxuries for himself and peace offerings for Helen. His generosity was as big as his swing at the plate. Babe gave freely to orphanages and hospitals, and he rarely turned down requests for donations, especially for causes that helped underprivileged kids. And he remembered his friends. He bought Brother Matthias a car, for example, and when it was totaled in a wreck,

All his life Babe loved kids, and often visited orphanages and children's hospitals like New York's Knickerbocker Hospital, 1930.

he bought him another one. When St. Mary's was destroyed in a fire in 1919 and had to close, it was the Babe who devised a plan to save it. He arranged for the St. Mary's band to travel as the Babe Ruth's Boys Band the following year with his team and take up collections. As a result, St. Mary's was able to rebuild the school.

Babe became a holdout before the 1919 season began. He had told Frazee that he wanted his salary doubled—from about $7,000 a year to $15,000. Only Ty Cobb was making more than that. And he wanted a two-year contract at that figure. On top of his monetary demands, Babe said he didn't want to pitch anymore.

Frazee, who had lost money during the preceding war-shortened season, said no. The Boston owner had already sold Ernie Shore, Duffy Lewis, and Dutch Leonard—three of the best Red Sox players—to the New York Yankees to earn some cash, and he wasn't about to pay Ruth that much money, even though he knew it was the Babe who kept Fenway Park filled with fans.

Ruth abruptly announced that if Frazee didn't meet his demands, he might retire from baseball altogether and become a full-time farmer. He even said he was thinking about switching from baseball to boxing. Frazee tried playing hardball with Ruth and refused to budge. But Ruth was nothing if not stubborn.

When the time came for the Red Sox to leave for spring training, Babe didn't even show up at the train station, and the team left without him. Frazee began to get worried. Finally they worked out an agreement for Ruth to get $10,000 a year for a three-year contract and an understanding that Babe would play only in left field. A preview of what the year would bring came in one of the first exhibition games of the year.

The Red Sox were playing the New York Giants at the Tampa Fairgrounds on a diamond laid out on the infield of a racetrack. In his first time at bat, Ruth smashed a home run that soared over the right fielder's head, over the infield fence, and across the track. Everyone turned and watched in awe. They had never seen a baseball hit so far. The Giants' right fielder marked the spot where the ball hit, and afterward they measured it. There was some confusion over where the ball landed and where it rolled after coming down. Some accounts said it went over 500 feet, others said over 600 feet. Barrow, who was there when they measured it, said it was 579 feet. Whatever the actual distance, it was the longest home run ever recorded at that time.

When the season opened, the Red Sox, who had now won three of the last four World Series, were once again favored to win it all. But troubles began the first week.

The team started the season on the road, and although Babe hit a home run on opening day in

New York, it became apparent to Ed Barrow, who was still managing the Red Sox, by the time they reached Washington that Ruth was staying out past curfew. Barrow bribed a hotel porter to come to his room and wake him the next night when Ruth finally got in. It was six A.M. when the porter knocked on the door to Barrow's room.

Barrow was furious. He threw on a robe and went to Ruth's room. When he entered, he saw Ruth in bed with the covers pulled up to his chin. He walked over and threw back the bedspread to find Ruth dressed in street clothes underneath the sheets.

"You're a fine citizen, Babe," Barrow said, fuming. "I must say, you're a fine citizen. I'll see you at the ballpark." Then he stalked out of the room.

Ruth slept for a few hours, then, as he prepared to go to the stadium for the day's game, he began to get angry. The more he thought about Barrow's barging into his room, the angrier he got. By the time he got to the stadium he was furious. When he saw Barrow in the clubhouse, he told the manager that if he ever came into his room like that again he would punch him in the nose. When he got really angry, Ruth's ultimate threat always seemed to be he would punch someone in the nose.

It took several players and Harry Hooper to keep the two men from fighting right then. Barrow went to the dugout on the field, and Ruth put on his uniform.

When Babe came into the dugout, he turned to Barrow and asked, "Am I playing today?"

"No," Barrow said. "No, you're not playing. And go inside and take off your uniform. You're suspended until further notice."

Oddly enough, Ruth meekly obeyed. He probably realized that he had stepped way over the line. After the game, which the Red Sox won, Ruth was quietly waiting for the rest of the team at Union Station. It had been the last game of the road trip, and the Red Sox were heading home to Boston. On board the train, Ruth knocked on Barrow's compartment and asked to talk to him.

The Babe was clearly contrite, and he began by apologizing. Then, possibly thinking of his father's death the previous year, he said, "Ed, someday, some-body is going to kill me."

Barrow relented. "Nobody's going to kill you, Babe. But don't you know you can't go around calling people names like that? What kind of bringing up did you have?"

Babe started to say something, but Barrow interrupted him. "I'm sorry, Babe, I forgot. I know you had it tough as a kid. But don't you think it's time you straightened out and started leading a decent life now? You can't go on the way you've been going."

Ruth agreed with his manager but said he didn't want somebody checking up on him all the time, like he was still at St. Mary's. The two agreed on a plan whereby Ruth would write a note with the time he got back to the hotel and leave it in Barrow's mailbox. The Babe was back in the lineup the next day.

Despite the peace treaty between Ruth and Barrow, the Red Sox began a long decline. The loss of Shore and Leonard had depleted their pitching staff from the start, and now with Ruth playing only left field, it was stretched even thinner by injuries to two other starters. Twice during the season, Ruth filled in for a few days in the starting rotation, but Barrow mostly honored the Babe's desire to play in the field.

By June, however, the team was in the second division, or the bottom half of the league standings, and it was clear there would be no pennant for the Red Sox that year. Ruth had pitched well when he pitched, and he had a 5–2 record by the end of June when he went back into left field. But what the Red Sox lost from Ruth on the mound, they more than gained from his daily appearance at the plate.

Although he had a slump at the beginning of the year, when he had been hitting .180, Ruth caught fire again. He raised his average to .325 in one month and started clouting the ball with such regularity that he became the focus of the first home-run record watch.

On July 5 he hit two home runs in one game for the first time, and he repeated the feat two weeks later in a game against Cleveland. In that game, the second one came in the ninth inning with the bases loaded, his second grand slam of the year. By the end of July, the Babe had hit 16 home runs, matching the American League record.

Home runs at that time were more of a curiosity than the big statistic they have become in present-day baseball. For one thing, they were harder to hit because the balls that were used in those days were softer than the ones used in the modern era. A player who hit 11 or 12 home runs in a season during those years could easily lead the league in that department.

Fans were now coming out to the stadium just to see if Ruth would hit another one, and sportswriters had already dubbed him the home-run king. After tying the American League record, he went two weeks without a homer. Then, on August 14, he belted one for number 17 and a new league mark.

Ruth got hot again. He hit three more homers in four games and was moving toward the major-league record of 27, which had been set in 1884 when the Chicago Colts had played on a diamond with a right-field fence only 215 feet from home plate. In the last week of August, Babe hit four in three days to bring his total for the year to 23.

For a Labor Day spectacular back in Fenway, it was announced Ruth would pitch the opening game of a doubleheader and play left field in the second. He won the opener 2–1, knocking in one run with a triple and scoring the winning run himself. Then in the second game he hit another home run, his twenty-fourth. Within the next few days, he hit two more, leaving him only one short of the all-time record.

For the next eleven days, baseball fans waited and waited, but Babe kept hitting singles and pop-ups. On September 20, the Red Sox announced that a double-header against Chicago would be Babe Ruth Day. He was scheduled to pitch the opener again. This time he ran into trouble in the sixth inning and was relieved, but he moved to left field. When he came up in the ninth inning, he hit a long home run to win the game and tie the record.

Ruth wasn't through, however. On the Red Sox' final road trip, he hit one more in New York and a final one in Washington to give him a total of 29 for the year, a new all-time home-run record. Four of his homers had been grand slams—another record for a season, and one that wouldn't be broken for forty years.

Although he didn't know it at the time, Babe had played his last game as a Red Sox. His season home-run record would only last one year. He would be the one to break it, with nearly twice as many, but he would be wearing a different uniform when he did it.

SEVEN

THE NEW YORK Yankees had been one of the weak sisters of the American League. Originally called the Highlanders, they had never won a pennant and were consistently in the second division when Jacob Ruppert and Tillinghast Huston, known as the two colonels, bought the club in 1915. Determined to turn the team into champions, they began by spending money to acquire good players. They had heard that the Red Sox owner was in need of ready cash. When he bought the team from Lannin, Frazee signed some promissory notes, and Lannin was now calling for payment. Frazee, who had other debts, was having trouble making them. Ruppert and Huston decided to make a bid for Ruth. Ruppert, Huston, and Frazee quickly reached a deal to send Ruth to the Yankees.

At the end of the previous season, Babe had gone

to California to play some exhibition baseball on the West Coast. There was no major-league team farther west than St. Louis in those days, and the only time fans in Los Angeles and San Francisco, for example, got to see the stars play was during tours in the fall, after the season ended.

The Yankees' manager, Miller Huggins, went all the way to California to tell Ruth the news before he read it in the newspapers. Babe said later that when he first saw Huggins in the lobby of his Los Angeles hotel, he knew he had been sold to the Yankees.

At their first meeting, Ruth began by asking for more money, and Huggins began by telling Babe he would have to behave himself if he came to New York. Ruth said that he was happy in Boston but that if he was traded to the Yankees, he would play as hard for them as he had for the Red Sox. The question of his behavior was left open.

The final terms of the deal that sent Babe Ruth to the New York Yankees were $100,000 in cash and a personal loan of $300,000 to Frazee from Ruppert. To secure the loan, the Red Sox owner put up Fenway Park for collateral.

◊ ◊ ◊

It would make a great fairy tale to report that Babe signed his contract and took the next train back to New York, and the Yankees immediately became a world champion baseball team. But it didn't happen that way.

In fact, Ruth stayed in California for another month, and when he went back east, he went to Boston. He and Helen spent the rest of the winter there, seeing friends and promoting his cigars. He staged one stunt in which he smoked three cigars at one time.

Everywhere he went in Boston, fans showered him with adulation, bemoaning the fact that he was no longer with the Red Sox. He was even honored with a testimonial dinner. The only person in Boston who refused to see him was Frazee, who was probably afraid the Babe might punch him in the nose.

Boston fans always blamed Frazee as the man who destroyed a great baseball team by selling its greatest player. The Red Sox finished dead last in nine of the next eleven seasons after they sold Ruth to the Yankees, and a legend built up that the team was jinxed. For decades afterward, every time the Red Sox came close to another World Series title, only to lose, fans said the curse of the Bambino was still on the team.

◊ ◊ ◊

Finally, the day came when he had to report to the
Yankees. He said good-bye to Helen and took a train
from Boston that got into Penn Station only ten minutes before the Yankees' team train was scheduled
to leave for Florida and spring training. Yet when
he arrived, a mob of New York fans were waiting for
him at the station, and in those ten minutes between
trains he became an instant hero. He walked through
the station grinning, joking, and shaking every hand
that was held out to him.

Even after he joined the team, the Babe's begin-
nings as a Yankee were something less than spectacular. By the end of the first month of the season, his new
owners began to wonder whether they had bought the
playboy Babe Ruth or the home-run Babe Ruth.

In Florida with the Yankees, he picked up where
he had left off with his partying. He was at the stadium
every day for practice, but at night he was nowhere to
be found. He deposited his suitcase in his hotel room,
but he only came there to change clothes. He was
assigned a room with a player named Ping Bodie, and
once when a reporter, trying to write a story about
the newest Yankee, asked Bodie what Babe Ruth was

really like, Bodie replied, "I don't know anything about him."

"You room with him," the reporter persisted. "What's he like when you're alone with him?"

"I don't room with him," Bodie said. "I room with his suitcase."

Ruth, by now twenty-five years old, had a good exhibition tour, but when the season began he was a dud. Fans were beginning to boo when he came to the plate. After all the hype in the media about his acquisition by the Yankees, Babe had not hit a single home run, and the Yankees were in the second division while the Red Sox were leading the league.

About the only thing Ruth acquired that first month as a Yankee was a new nickname. Because many of the Yankee fans came from the large population of Italian immigrants in New York, his name of Babe was translated by them into the Italian word for baby—*bambino*. It quickly took hold, and the newspapers even shortened it in their headlines to "Bam." Babe Ruth. The Bambino. Bam.

He had many nicknames over the course of his career, some of them not very complimentary or nice.

Newspapers called him the Bronx Bomber or the Sultan of Swat. Another name answered to was "Jedge," a deliberate mispronunciation of "George," and that was the one by which he was most frequently known for some years in the Yankee clubhouse.

If Babe was unpredictable at the plate, he was equally impulsive in his behavior. It was as though his fiery temper and his innate good-natured humor were in a constant struggle, and everyone around him held their breath waiting to see which would emerge.

Two stories from those first weeks as a Yankee tell the difference. Once during Ruth's dismal start, a spectator in the front row began heckling him. Ruth, like most ballplayers, had learned to take boos from the fans in stride. But this man kept needling Ruth all afternoon, calling him "every kind of bum he could think of," as Ruth later told it. Ruth's anger kept rising, and finally he decided he'd had enough. He climbed over the railing into the stands and started for the guy. The man pulled a long knife and began waving it at the Babe. Some other players pulled Ruth away, and the man ran off.

The Babe's lighter side came out after his first

game in center field. Ruth told Huggins at the end of spring training that he wanted to switch from left field to center. Huggins agreed, and in his debut at the position, on opening day, Ruth dropped an easy fly ball that let in two opposing runs. The error lost the game for the Yankees. One of the players for the other side decided to tease Ruth and found an old brown derby hat, which in those days was regarded as a sort of dunce cap. He wrapped it up and had it delivered to Ruth at home plate the next afternoon when he came to bat in the first inning.

Babe stepped out of the batter's box, unwrapped the parcel, and stared at the hat. The fans, the opposing team, even the umpire, all began laughing. The other Yankee players, watching from the dugout, held their breath, afraid he might explode in anger. But the Babe held up the hat and put it on his head. When it came down over his eyes, he began to mug at home plate, groping around like a blind man. The crowd went wild.

The Babe's career as the Bronx Bomber finally began on May 1, 1920. He hit his first home run of the season, a towering drive that went all the way over the roof at the Polo Grounds, as the Yankees shut out the Red Sox, 6–0. By the end of the month, Ruth had hit 12 homers and the Yankees had climbed to the top of the standings.

In June, Ruth hit 12 more homers, and by the middle of July he was batting .385 and had tied his own home-run record of 29, set the year before. Fans were streaming into stadiums all around the league just to watch Ruth hit. By this time, he was being intentionally walked almost as many times as he was allowed to hit (he had 148 walks that season, most of them intentional), and fans in opposing cities would boo their own pitchers when they would give Ruth a base on balls.

Attendance at baseball games had increased considerably since the end of World War I, but there was an explosion of interest in 1920, and the Babe was the main cause of it. The Yankees, who had always played second fiddle to the New York Giants at the Polo Grounds, outdrew their landlords that year and became the first major-league team to draw over a million customers (1,289,422, to be exact) in a season.

The fact that the Yankees outdrew the Giants in

the Giants' home stadium so infuriated the Giants' owners that they issued an eviction notice to the Yankees at the Polo Grounds. The Yankees would have to play somewhere else. There was no rush, the Giants said, but they would have to leave as soon as possible. The Yankee owners bought some land in the Bronx just across the Harlem River from the Polo Grounds, and in the spring they began building a new stadium that would hold nearly twice as many fans.

After all, Ruth was giving all those new Yankee fans something to cheer about. He had a phenomenal first year. By the end of the 1920 season he had whacked 54 home runs. He batted .376 on the year, with a slugging average of .847. He scored 158 runs and had 137 RBIs. The American League pennant, which had been the goal when Ruppert and Huston bought Ruth, would have to wait a year. But the Yankees were in the chase for it until the final week of the season.

It was also at the end of that 1920 season that the scandal of the Chicago Black Sox broke open. A Chicago grand jury began investigating reports that several players on the Chicago team had sold out to a group of professional gamblers and had fixed the 1919 World Series, which Chicago lost to Cincinnati. In his autobiography, Ruth recalled:

> To me, it was like hearing that my Church had sold out. I couldn't comprehend how any Big League players could defraud not only the millions of fans all over the country, but millions of kids, by throwing the biggest sporting event of the year.

The scandal, which resulted in eight players on the Chicago team, including Shoeless Joe Jackson, being banished from the sport for life, was felt the following year at stadium box offices across the country. Followers of America's pastime felt cheated, and the game of baseball was tarnished forever in the eyes of many of them. But by having an incredible season that topped his previous one, Babe helped restore many fans' confidence in baseball.

In contrast to his first year as a Yankee, Ruth began the 1921 season like a man on a mission. And perhaps he was. He had hit five home runs by the end of April, and he kept swinging for the fences through the rest of the summer. He started out hitting .400 in those first few weeks, and his batting average stayed around .380 for the whole season. He ended up with 59 home runs for the year, breaking his own mark set the previous season.

The Yankees clinched their first American League pennant with days to spare. Ruth badgered Huggins into letting him pitch in a meaningless game late in the season. In the eighth inning he came in, with the Yankees winning 6–0. But the Babe immediately gave up six runs, tying the score. Huggins, however, left Ruth on the mound, and Babe pitched shutout ball for the next three innings. The Yankees eventually won the game 7–6 in the eleventh inning. Ruth got credit for the win, making him 3–0 as a Yankee pitcher. He would pitch only twice more in his career—in 1930 and 1933—each time at the end of the season in an effort to boost attendance. He won both of those games, too.

The Giants, now being challenged by the Yankees as New York's favorite team, won the National League pennant. The entire 1921 World Series, which was then a best-of-nine series, was going to be played between two New York teams at the Polo Grounds. The Yankees won the first two games, and it looked like they would take the Series easily. Giant pitchers walked Ruth three times in the second game, and perhaps out of frustration, he stole second base standing up, then stole third base sliding.

However, Ruth scraped his elbow sliding into third, and the injury developed into an infection. He played in the fourth game, but the infection got worse and turned into an abscess that had to be lanced. Babe was again in the lineup the following day, but his arm was bandaged, and although he hit a home run—his first in World Series play—he was clearly uncomfortable at the plate.

The injury was not healing, and there was genuine concern that his infected arm might develop into blood poisoning. The doctor warned him that if that happened, he might face amputation of his arm. Ruth did not even suit up for the next two games. The Yankees fell behind the Giants, and although Ruth was in uniform for the final game, he did not play. He went in to pinch-hit in the ninth inning, but he grounded out, and the Giants won the game and the Series five games to three. The Babe had the off-season to let his arm heal. The Yankees, however, had won their first pennant, and for their fans, it was only a taste of the glory that was to come.

The 1922 season was one that almost didn't happen for the Babe. One of the results of the Black Sox scandal was the emergence of Kenesaw Mountain Landis, a former judge, as the solitary commissioner of baseball. From then on Judge Landis ruled over the sport as a sort of dictator. It was Landis who banished the Chicago players for life, and it was Landis who decided to enforce a rule that forbade players from World Series teams from playing exhibition ball after the season ended.

The rule had been on the books for years, but no one until Landis had tried to enforce it. Many players counted on picking up some money in the off-season on the tours that went to small towns that did not otherwise see major-league baseball. Ruth, always in need of money, was not about to let Landis stop him.

Ruth and several players had signed a deal to play exhibition ball in Pennsylvania, upstate New York, and all the way to Oklahoma, as a team called the Babe Ruth All Stars. When Landis heard about the plans, he called Ruth on the telephone and warned him not to go on the tour. The Babe told him he had already signed the contracts, and he was going to play the first game the next day in Buffalo.

"Oh, you are, are you?" Landis snapped. "If you do, it will be the sorriest thing you've ever done in base-ball." The commissioner slammed down the phone and fumed to a sportswriter who was in his office, "Who does that big monkey think he is? It seems I'll have to show somebody who's running this game."

The Yankees, afraid of what Landis might do, tried to talk Babe out of making the trip. "Tell the old guy to go jump in a lake," Babe said, and caught the train to Buffalo.

The issue came to a head when the Babe Ruth All Stars played their first game. Now Landis was in a tight spot. He would face the wrath of fans across the country if he tried to banish Babe Ruth from base-ball. On the other hand, his own authority had been openly challenged.

In the end, the Babe Ruth All Stars played their

tour, and Judge Landis backed away from trying to ban Ruth from baseball. He did, however, withhold Ruth's share of the World Series money and suspend him for the first six weeks of the 1922 season.

On top of the suspension, Ruth's contract had expired, and the Yankee owners took the train to Hot Springs to negotiate a new one. The Babe had gone to Hot Springs at the end of his tour to play golf, go to the horse races and casinos, and have a good time in general. Ruth kept turning down every figure the Yankee bosses threw at him, but when a final offer of $50,000 a year for five years was made, the Babe countered, "Make it fifty-two thousand and it's a deal."

Huston stared at him. "All right, agreed," he said. "But why fifty-*two* thousand?"

"Well," Ruth said. "There are fifty-two weeks in the year, and I've always wanted to make a grand a week."

Although Ruth's $52,000 salary may seem like peanuts in today's megamillion market for baseball players, it was by far the most money any baseball player had ever been paid at that time. To put it in perspective, the closest any other player earned that year was $16,000. The Babe was bringing in over three times that amount.

There was no television money to help pay for players' salaries in those days, and team owners had to depend on customers coming to the stadium to make money. Still, more people paid to see Babe Ruth play baseball than any other player, and both the Yankee owners and the Babe knew it.

Despite his new contract, the 1922 season was one the Babe probably would rather have forgot. Because of the suspension, Ruth didn't play a game until May 20. Some forty thousand fans showed up for his first game, and the Babe totally flopped. He struck out, popped up twice, and grounded out. And that was only the beginning of a terrible start.

By this time, there had been so much hyperbole written about the Babe that every time he didn't get a hit, the fans began to boo him. Baseball fans can change direction faster than the wind. During his first week, fans jeered Ruth every time he came up to the plate. The boos only increased every time he made an out. But when he hit his first home run of the season, later in the week, the crowd cheered him around the bases.

It was clear, however, that the Babe was in a slump. By the end of the month he was batting less than .100, and the fans seemed to have as much fun booing him as they did when he was hitting home runs. They would even boo him in the field. At the start, the Babe took it all in stride, and he would even tip his cap to the stands. But the catcalls and jeering soon began to burn him, and it all boiled over in one game at the Polo Grounds.

Ruth hit a single to center field, but he tried to stretch it into a double and was thrown out at second base. The Babe leapt to his feet and began arguing with the umpire. He reached down, picked up some dirt, and threw it at the ump, who immediately ejected Ruth from the game. As he was walking off the field a fan yelled, "You big bum, why don't you play ball." Ruth jumped up on the dugout and headed into the stands to punch the guy in the nose. Fans separated them, but Ruth got another suspension.

During the summer, Ruth again got involved in an argument with an umpire and used some profanity, and he was suspended again. When he came back, he appeared chastened, and he started hitting well. Toward the end of summer, he got into another argument after being called out on strikes, and was ejected and again suspended for several days. Over the course of the season, Ruth was suspended four times—a major-league record and one the Babe was not proud to own.

Despite all the turbulence, the Yankees again won the American League pennant and again played the Giants in the World Series. The Babe's troubles persisted, and he had only one hit in seventeen trips to the plate. This was also the year that the Series was shortened to the best of seven, and the Giants swept the Yankees in four straight games.

A curious footnote to that stormy year came at the end of the season when Helen, now twenty-five years old, showed up after a brief absence with a sixteen-month-old baby girl named Dorothy. When reporters asked her about it, she insisted it was her own baby and said it had been born at St. Vincent's Hospital in New York the previous June. When pressed on why no one had seen the baby for the past sixteen months, she said it had been with a nurse.

Ruth, who was on the road when the little girl appeared, was also asked about it. He said it had been born the previous February at Presbyterian Hospital in New York. He said the baby had been very small and he and Helen had not announced it at the time because they didn't want a lot of publicity. However, reporters found no birth record at either St. Vincent's or Presbyterian in either June or February.

In her will, after her death, Helen referred to Dorothy as an adopted daughter. Yet reporters also never found any official adoption papers for the girl. Dorothy herself said years later that she was Ruth's natural daughter, born to one of his girlfriends and taken to be raised by Helen and Babe as their own. At the time of her appearance, however, Dorothy was only one more piece of what had been a bizarre puzzle of a year.

During the year, when Ruth seemed to get into one scrape after another, the Yankees, as the club did several times during the Babe's career, asked Brother Matthias to come and talk to him. He did, and it helped Babe settle down. He would be twenty-eight years old the following February, and Brother Matthias told him he had to start acting like a man.

After the season ended, Ruth's new manager, Christy Walsh, suggested he hold a dinner party with some of the New York sportswriters and leading citizens and try to improve his image. At the dinner party, Ruth sat and listened to Jimmy Walker, the future mayor of New York, chastise him for his behavior and for letting down "the kids of America." At the end of the evening Ruth, tears in his eyes, made a speech in which he apologized for his behavior during the season and pledged to go to his farm in Sudbury (which he and Helen had kept even after he moved to New York) and work hard, and he would be a new man by next spring.

Mostly, he kept his word. He worked at remodeling the farmhouse and he worked at losing some weight, which was beginning to be a perennial problem for him. When he reported for the 1923 season, he was trimmer than he had been in years, and it showed at the plate.

Babe started out hitting that season, and he kept it up all year long. The Yankees walked away with the pennant for the third straight time and once again faced the Giants in the World Series. But this year they would be playing in different ballparks.

Yankee Stadium opened this year, and more than 62,000 fans jammed into it for the first game played there. It had cost the owners $2.5 million to build and was a state-of-the-art ballpark that would last over eighty years. Ruppert and Huston were not overly concerned about the price, because they counted on fans filling it for years to come to watch Ruth. Since the ballpark had been built partly with money they had made from fans who had paid to come see him, the stadium came to be known almost immediately as The House That Ruth Built.

Ruth contributed his part to the history of the stadium by hitting a home run on opening day for the new field. There was even talk at the time of naming it Ruth Stadium, but during his days as a player the only part of it that bore his name was the right-field bleachers, where he hit most of his home runs, which became known to fans as Ruthville.

In addition to the new stadium, there were other changes in the Yankees that year. Ruppert bought out Huston shortly after the stadium was opened to become the sole principal owner, and Ed Barrow, Ruth's old manager from the Red Sox, was brought in as general manager of the team.

Throughout the season, Babe certainly made

good on his promise of the previous fall. He was a reformed man on the field, and his focus paid off with the bat. He hit .393 on the year, clobbered 41 home runs—modest, perhaps, by his own standards, but still a dozen more than his closest rival—and led the league in RBIs. He had 205 hits on the year, nearly half of them for extra bases. It was a startling number considering that he also was walked 170 times, mostly intentionally. Once he was even walked intentionally with the bases loaded, the opposing team preferring to give up a single run rather than risk Ruth hitting a grand slam.

It was also in 1923 that the Yankees finally broke the spell of the Giants and won their first World Championship. The Giants took a 2–1 lead in the Series, mainly on a pair of home runs by a young Casey Stengel, but the Yankees won the last three games behind three home runs from Ruth.

The reformed Ruth carried over into the 1924 season as well, although the Yankees were edged out for the American League pennant by the Washington Senators. Babe, however, hit .378 on the year to win his first and only batting title, and he added another

46 home runs—19 more than his nearest rival—to his growing total.

Although there had been no more suspensions or serious altercations with umpires or fans, there was trouble brewing in the Babe's private life that would reach a crisis the following season.

EIGHT

THROUGHOUT HER MARRIAGE to Babe, Helen had mostly turned a blind eye to his escapades with other women. At the start, Babe's philandering mostly occurred during out-of-town road trips, and he took pains to hide it from his young wife. But over the years, his almost pathological pursuit of women became more open, and he would often spend the night away from home even when the team was in town.

Helen, of course, heard all the rumors about Babe and other women, and she was hurt by it. The two began to argue more often, and in public. Babe's bad behavior tended to follow a pattern. He would go out with some of the guys for drinks after a game, drink too much, eat too much, and end up spending the night with some woman. After a time, Babe would begin to feel guilty and contrite and try to straighten up. But then the cycle would start to repeat.

The issue over women became more serious when Babe began regularly seeing a woman named Claire Hodgson. In the past, most of his encounters with women had been one-night stands, but this was different. Babe first met Claire a couple of years earlier, but they did not become romantically involved until that winter after the 1924 season.

At the age of fourteen, Claire had married a wealthy man who was over twice her age. It had not worked out, and she had moved from her native Georgia to New York with her baby daughter, Julia. When her husband died a few years later, Claire became a beautiful and rich young widow. Claire had been a model and had appeared in some revues on Broadway and the Ziegfeld Follies.

Babe fell in love with Claire and began to spend as much time with her as possible. Celebrity scandals were not headlines in those days, especially with sportswriters, who didn't want to anger the players they had to write about. But players' off-field behavior was beginning to gain more newspaper attention, and Ruth's affair with Claire was so open, it was impossible for either the reporters or Helen to ignore it.

At one point, when the Yankees were on a road trip, Helen was asked about the New York widow that Ruth had been seen with in public. "I don't care to talk on that subject for publication," Helen said, bristling at the question. "However, I intend to discuss these matters with my husband when he returns."

She did, and the result was that she and Ruth separated. Since they were both Catholic, divorce was out of the question, and a priest even arranged a reconciliation between them. But it was only a temporary solution.

Babe's tumultuous private life, meanwhile, began to be mirrored on the baseball diamond. As spring rolled around, Babe prepared to report to the Yankees' training camp. Before going to Florida, however, he returned to Hot Springs, a place he had always liked from his first spring training there with the Baltimore Orioles. He could eat, drink, play golf, and run around all he wanted. The Roaring Twenties were in full swing, and although Prohibition was then in force, there was not a bootlegger or a speakeasy in the country that would not give Babe Ruth a drink if he wanted it. Ruth might take a steam bath every day in

Hot Springs, and jog a little, but otherwise he took little care of himself.

By the time Ruth, who was now thirty years old, got to Florida for spring training, he weighed over 250 pounds and was suffering from a bad cold. In fact, he was running a fever of over 105 degrees, and his stomach was in open rebellion against all the food and drink he was cramming into it. Helen joined him during spring training, and he behaved himself and got better. When the team left camp to start the exhibition tour back north, Helen returned home, and Babe went wild.

In town after town, Babe would play ball in the afternoon, then go out at night in search of a party. Miller Huggins had no control over him, and the Babe, who always called the Yankee manager "the flea," paid no attention to his admonitions. In fact, there was no love lost between Ruth and Huggins, and Babe broke curfew almost every night despite the manager's orders for all players to be in the hotel by one A.M. Babe started the exhibition season hitting well, batting .447 despite the fact that as a team, the Yankees were playing poorly.

But Ruth's abuse to his body took its toll. His weight ballooned to over 270 pounds, and what was described as a cold returned, again with a high temperature. Still, he tried to play every day. The situation reached a crisis in early April in North Carolina.

Ruth's fever got so bad that he was walking around in a sweat. "I'm burning up," he said. "Every bone in my body aches." It was agreed Babe should return to New York and try to get well by opening day. But at the train station, Babe collapsed. He was taken back to the hotel, and a local doctor said he had a severe intestinal problem. The following day he was helped onto a train bound for New York.

The trip went well until the end, when Babe again passed out in the men's washroom. By the time the train pulled into Penn Station, an ambulance had been ordered to take him to St. Vincent's Hospital. Helen was there to meet him, but when the orderlies brought a stretcher to take him off the train, he began to go into convulsions and fought the medics, who had to sedate him. Helen rode with him in the ambulance.

Once he was in the hospital, doctors discovered he

had an intestinal abscess and would have to undergo surgery. It was performed the next day and was a success, although it left Babe with a six-inch scar across his stomach. Newspapers followed the drama daily, and one called his illness "the bellyache heard round the world." But it was a bellyache that left him hospitalized for seven weeks.

When he finally returned to the team at the end of May, the Yankees suggested he take more time to recover from the surgery. But Babe was eager to start playing again, and the Yankees, who were in seventh place in the standings, could use his bat. He was in the starting lineup on June 1, but he aggravated the wound in his stomach sliding headfirst into third base, and was on and off the sick list for the rest of the year. Sportswriters were already saying that Ruth would never be the superstar he had been in past years.

In fact, the Babe was a mess through most of 1925. During one slump, Huggins sent in another batter to pinch-hit for Ruth. On the road, he was as uncontrollable as his bat was at the plate. In every town, he would stay out half the night, looking for women or partying. He and Helen had another brief separation in the summer, and she returned to the farm in Sudbury. Once again, they briefly patched things up. But the truth was that Babe and Helen rarely saw each other, and the presence of Dorothy as a daughter had not had the stabilizing effect on him that Helen had hoped. Ruth was not only an absent husband, he was also an absent father.

The short fuse that Babe had been on all season burned out toward the end of the summer, and the explosion that followed almost ended his career. In the long run, it may have saved him.

Huggins had been on a slow burn about the Babe's behavior all year, and the final straw came in St. Louis in August. Ruth stayed out all night two nights in a row, not even returning to the hotel before reporting to the ballpark. On the second of those nights, all the other players were dressed and on the field when Babe came into the clubhouse. Huggins was waiting for him.

"Don't bother getting dressed, Babe," he said. "You're not playing today."

Ruth didn't say a word but put on his jacket and started to leave.

"I'm suspending you," Huggins went on. "And I'm fining you $5,000. You're to go back to New York on the five o'clock train."

Ruth blew up. He fumed and shouted and called Huggins every name he could think of and said if Huggins was even half his size, he would punch him in the nose. The manager, who had already told Barrow and Ruppert in advance what he planned to do and had received their blessing, stood his ground. Ruth stormed out and left the team.

But Babe did not take the five o'clock train to New York that day. Instead he took the noon train to Chicago the following day, vowing to appeal in person to Judge Landis, the baseball commissioner. By that time, Ruth's fine and suspension were headline news, and reporters followed him everywhere. In Ruth's view, his behavior was hardly a reason for a $5,000 fine and suspension, and he expressed confidence that Judge Landis would understand and reinstate him. Babe had other things to say to the reporters as well. He blamed Huggins for the dismal year the Yankees were having and threatened to leave the team if Huggins stayed on as manager.

"I'm through with them," Babe said. "I won't be playing with them next year if Huggins is still there. Either he quits or I quit, because I'll never play for him again."

Judge Landis refused to see Ruth officially, saying it was an internal Yankee matter. Babe then took a train to New York, saying he would take his case to Ruppert, who, he was sure, would understand and order Huggins to lift the suspension and fine.

In the meantime, however, Ruppert had issued his own statement backing his manager. "I'm behind Huggins to the limit," Ruppert told reporters. "There will be no remission of the fine, and the suspension will last as long as Huggins wants it to last. . . . Huggins will be manager as long as he wants to be manager."

By the time Babe arrived in Grand Central Terminal in New York, he had calmed down considerably. Perhaps he had been told about Ruppert's statement, or maybe he had realized that he had gone too far. But he began a slow retreat from the threats he had made about not playing for the Yankees if Huggins was manager. "I guess I was a little too rash," he said. "I don't want to be traded. New York is my city."

On top of it all, Babe learned when he got back to New York that Helen had suffered a nervous breakdown and been hospitalized. She had had bouts of nervous problems in the past, but they had never been this serious. Ruth went straight to the hospital to see her, and they had a tearful reunion in her room, which was duly recorded by newspaper photographers. Ruth then went to see Ruppert. They met in private for a long time, and when they came out to meet reporters, Ruth was strangely silent. When a reporter asked him if he had been reinstated, it was Ruppert who answered:

No, he is not reinstated. The fine and the suspension stand. I told Ruth, as I tell you now in front of him, that he went too far. I told him Miller Huggins is in absolute command of the ball club, and that I stand behind Huggins to the very limit. I told him it is up to him to see Huggins, admit his errors and apologize for his hot-headedness. It is up to him to reinstate himself.

As he left the meeting, a reporter asked Ruth if he would go to see Huggins. "Yes, of course," the Babe said. "Maybe we can get this settled."

But apologizing to Huggins proved more difficult than the Babe at first imagined. Ruth went straight from Ruppert's office to Yankee Stadium, but when he went into the clubhouse, Huggins ignored him. Ruth asked if he could play that day, and Huggins told him no. Ruth asked if they could talk things over, and Huggins told him no. Huggins said he would let Babe know when he was ready to talk.

For the next several days, Babe kept coming to the stadium and asking to speak to Huggins. But the manager kept putting him off, saying he wasn't ready to talk. It was nearly a week before Huggins allowed a by now humbled and contrite Babe to apologize, in front of the whole team, and restored him to the lineup. But the Babe's return didn't help the Yankees in 1925. It was a miserable year for the team, which finished next to last in the standings, but Ruth and Huggins never had a serious feud again. And Babe Ruth was on the brink of his greatest glory days.

In his autobiography, Ruth confessed that he had "acted like a spoiled child" during his run-in with Huggins. "I am not proud of this chapter of my baseball life," Ruth said. "It is one of those things a man would like to change if he could alter the past. But men and boys learn from experience, and I believe I learned something from this one."

Ruth did indeed appear to have learned something when he reported for spring training the following year. He spent a lot of that off-season working out at Artie McGovern's gym in New York, and he was in the best shape he had been in years when he showed up in Florida for training camp.

It was also during that off-season, however, that Helen and Babe had their final separation, and this time it was for good. Helen moved back to Boston, and they put the farm in Sudbury up for sale. They never lived together again, and Dorothy stayed with Helen.

For many baseball historians, the Yankees of the next three years—the 1926, 1927, and 1928 seasons—were among the best baseball teams ever fielded. Huggins and Ruth, if not exactly bosom buddies, were on good terms and focused on bringing the American League pennant back to the roof of Yankee Stadium.

There were no more suspensions or fines or long periods on the disabled list for Ruth. He was now thiry-one years old, and he played nearly every game in 1926. He batted .372, hit 47 homers, and had 155 RBIs. He was unanimously named Most Valuable Player, oddly enough the only year he ever achieved that honor. Ruth also had some help. The previous season the Yankees had signed a young player named Lou Gehrig, and he was beginning to look like the extra star they had hoped for.

The Yankees started as if they would run away with the title, winning 16 straight games early in the season. They led the standings by 10 games at the start of September but faced a late-season challenge from Cleveland. Still, they won by three games, and the team that was near the cellar the year before was again the American League champion.

The turnaround in Ruth that year was remarkable in every way. At one point toward the end of the season, Huggins told him: "Babe, I admire a man who can win over a lot of tough opponents, but I admire even more a man who can win over himself."

"That's fine, Hug," Ruth rejoined. "Do I get my fine back?"

"No," the manager replied.

But Babe was gratified by his manager's words and had praise of his own for Huggins. "I really was beginning to become very fond of little Hug and had more respect for him than ever before," he said. "I always admired him for the way he was able to pick up that seventh-place 1925 club and in one year whip it into another pennant winner."

The World Series put the Yankees against the St. Louis Cardinals, and the two teams fought evenly through six games. In the seventh and deciding game, the Cardinals were leading by one run in the bottom of the ninth when Ruth was intentionally walked by the veteran pitcher Grover Cleveland Alexander. For reasons only he knew, Ruth tried to steal second with Gehrig on deck. He was thrown out, and the Series was over. Although he had hit four home runs during the Series, Ruth ended up being the goat.

But the Yankees were on the verge of becoming a powerhouse. The 1927 season was one of the most memorable in baseball. Ruth said later in his life that

When Lou Gehrig (left) joined the Yankees, he and Ruth became close friends and batted back-to-back in the lineup.

it was the greatest team he ever played on. It was also the year that saw the first great home-run battle, and this one was between two teammates—Ruth and Gehrig.

Through the first half of the year, Ruth and Gehrig matched home run for home run, and by the middle of August, Gehrig was even ahead of Ruth with 38 homers to Ruth's 35. But then the Babe started to pull ahead. Gehrig's bat cooled off while Ruth's got even hotter. There was yet another home-run watch, as fans and sportswriters speculated on whether Ruth could break his own record of 59.

By the middle of September, the Babe had hit 50, and with only 17 games left to play, it seemed doubtful that he could match his 1921 total. He hit three more over the course of one week, but he still needed seven to break the record, and there were only nine games left to play. He did not hit any homers in the next two games, and it looked like his record was safe. Then he hit three in three straight games. That left him with four to go in four games.

The next day he hit a grand slam, and added two more in one game the following afternoon, tying his old mark. He now had two games to get one more home run for a new record. He got it in the next-to-last day of the season, a sharp shot down the right field line that just cleared the foul pole. Tom Zachary, the pitcher who served up the sixtieth home run, claimed it was a foul ball and argued with the umpire. But Ruth had the record.

The Yankees won 110 games and lost only 44 that year. It wasn't just that they won. They murdered their opponents. The team scored 975 runs over the course of the 154-game season, an average of more than six runs a game. Ruth had 164 RBIs on the year and scored 158. Gehrig batted in 175 and scored 149. No one could beat them. They won 21 out of 21 games against the St. Louis Browns, until the Browns won the last one of the season. The Yankees won the pennant by 19 games and swept the World Series from the Pittsburgh Pirates four games to none.

Ruth credited Gehrig with helping him hit his 60 home runs. Gehrig had been moved up to bat fourth in the Yankee lineup, just behind Ruth. That meant

Babe Ruth is most remembered as the Yankees' home run king. On Sept. 30, 1927, he hit his record sixtieth in one season.

that Ruth got fewer intentional walks—if an opposing pitcher walked Babe, he had to face Gehrig—and more opportunities to swing the bat.

Ruth and Gehrig could not have been more opposite personalities. Gehrig, who was eight years younger than Ruth, lived at home with his mother and was a quiet, unassuming man, modest in his habits. Ruth lived wherever he dropped his hat for the night and was garrulous and excessive in everything he did. Yet the two men became very close friends through most of their careers.

The 1928 season picked up where the old one left off. The Yankees again started like a house on fire, and by the middle of summer they were leading the league by 13 and a half games. Then injuries began to hit the team, and they sputtered through the last half of the season, and by the middle of September the young Philadelphia Athletics, which would later move first to Kansas City and then to Oakland, caught them and went ahead.

The A's were leading the league by a half game when they came into Yankee Stadium for a four-game series. The first two games were a doubleheader. The stands were packed, and thousands of fans were turned away at the gates. New York won both games. The following day, the Babe hit a two-run homer in the eighth inning to break a tie, and the Yankees wrapped up their third straight American League pennant.

It was the second time in eight years that the Yankees had won three straight titles, and they followed the 1928 title with another World Series sweep, this time over the Cardinals, getting revenge for their Series defeat two years earlier.

On the season, Babe hit 54 home runs—the fourth time he had hit more than 50. He batted .625 during the four-game Series, and six of his ten hits were for extra bases. In one game, he hit three home runs—the second time he had hit three homers in one World Series game. He even made a spectacular catch of a foul ball in the left-field stands for the last St. Louis out.

It was a benchmark of his career and established the Yankees as a powerhouse baseball club. They had won six pennants in eight years and had won back-to-back World Series without losing a game—eight straight Series victories.

NINE

THE YEAR 1929 started off with a disaster for Ruth, and it didn't get much better, either for him, the Yankees, or the rest of the country.

In January, a fire burned down a house in the Boston suburb of Watertown. A woman was found dead in the charred remains of the fire, and neighbors said it was the wife of the owner, a dentist named Edward Kinder. Dr. Kinder had not been home at the time the fire broke out, and a little girl whom neighbors had assumed was the couple's daughter was also away.

As it turned out, however, the victim of the fire was not Dr. Kinder's wife but rather Helen Ruth, the estranged wife of baseball's superstar. After finally separating from Babe three years earlier, Helen had begun a relationship with the dentist, whom she had known during her childhood in South Boston, and ended up living with him in Watertown. The girl neighbors thought was their daughter was Dorothy, the baby Helen had adopted and tried to pass off as her own, who was now six years old.

Babe burst into tears when he learned about Helen's death and took the next train to Boston. The mysterious circumstances surrounding the fire and the identity of the victim led Helen's family to issue some wild charges, suggesting that there had been foul play and the fire was not an accident. This prompted the Boston medical examiner to perform an autopsy, and Helen's funeral was delayed pending its outcome.

Ruth stayed in Boston and avoided reporters who were hounding him for some comment about the unusual turn of events. It was only after Helen was buried that Babe met reporters in his hotel suite.

"I hold nothing against my wife," he said, tears in his eyes. "She was the victim of circumstances. I still love her. I have fine memories of her. What I'm going to say I can say in very few words. Please leave my wife alone. Let her stay dead. That's all I'm going to say."

Reporters persisted in trying to ask questions, but the Babe said no more. When one asked about Dorothy, he replied, "I'd rather not say anything about the little girl." The truth was Babe had rarely, if ever, seen Dorothy since he and Helen separated.

But Babe had plans for Dorothy. Three months after Helen's death, Babe and Claire married, and after a few months in which she was in foster care, he brought Dorothy to live with them. In an unusual arrangement, Claire formally adopted Dorothy, and

Ruth in a family picture with his wife, Claire, and their daughters, Dorothy and Julia, each from previous relationships, 1930.

Babe adopted Julia, Claire's daughter from her first marriage, so the two girls were raised from then on as legally sisters.

The Yankees had hoped to make it four straight American League titles in 1929. But a series of injuries crippled the team, including some to Ruth that kept him out of the lineup for several weeks, and by Labor Day the Yankees were already out of the race. But that was not the biggest loss they would face that year.

Huggins, their manager, became noticeably ill as the team went through its decline. Always a small man, he almost stopped eating, and his eyes seemed to shrink back in his face. He developed a small sore under one eye, and when he finally went to have it checked by a doctor, he learned that he was suffering from a bacterial blood infection. It was a kind of poisoning, and Huggins died five days later. He was forty-nine years old.

The Yankees were playing in Boston at the time, and when news of the manager's death reached them, the Babe broke down and cried in the clubhouse. The team was all present at Huggins's funeral service at the Little Church Around the Corner in New York, and Ruth again wept.

There were several games left to play in the season, and Art Fletcher, one of the team's coaches, took over the manager's job for the remainder of it. Everyone assumed he would be named to succeed Huggins the following year. Ruppert indeed offered him the job, but Fletcher turned it down, saying he preferred to stay as coach.

That planted an idea in Babe's head that eventually would lead to friction between him and Ruppert and cloud his last seasons as a Yankee. With no clear candidate on the horizon to succeed Huggins as manager, Babe decided he should have the job and approached Ruppert about it. After all, there were other examples of player-managers, even among the game's superstars. Ty Cobb had managed while continuing to play; so had Tris Speaker and Rogers Hornsby.

Ruppert pretended to take the Babe's request seriously and told him he would think it over and call him in a couple of days. A week later, Ruth picked up a paper and read the headline that Bob Shawkey, another of the Yankees' coaches, had been named to manage the club in 1930. Babe and Shawkey got along all right, but Ruth was upset over how Ruppert had handled things, and he decided he would make the Yankee owner pay in another way.

Babe's contract was up that year, and when the Yankee owner offered to renew at $70,000 a year he rejected it. Ruth said he wanted $100,000. Ruppert rejected that. They traded numbers back and forth but were still $5,000 apart on the eve of the exhibition season. Ruth was ready to play without a contract until someone asked him what he would do if he got injured. Then Ruppert wouldn't have to pay him anything.

Ruth quickly agreed to the owner's last offer—$80,000 a year for two years—and signed the contract just before the umpire shouted "play ball" for the first game.

Herbert Hoover was president of the United States, and he had watched America collapse from the 1929 stock market crash into the beginning of the Great Depression. At that time, the president earned a salary of $75,000 a year, and a reporter asked Ruth if he thought he should be paid more than Hoover. "Why not," he said. "I had a better year than he did."

Ruth also had a pretty good year in 1930, hitting 49 homers, batting .359, and driving in 153 runs. But the Yankees as a team did not, finishing third in the standings. Shawkey was fired after one season, and Babe renewed his request to be named manager.

Ruppert, however, was no more sympathetic to the proposition than he had been the previous year. In addition, Ed Barrow, the Yankees' general manager and the man whose advice Ruppert followed, was dead set against Ruth becoming team manager, possibly as a result of the wildness he had endured from Ruth when he managed him in Boston.

The Yankee owner gave Ruth a hearing, then listed all the scrapes and wild escapades he had been in during his younger days as a Red Sox and a Yankee. Ruth, who was now thirty-five years old, countered that he had been a good citizen the past few years, and that he knew more about pitching and hitting than any other candidate. But it became clear to Ruth that Ruppert had somebody else in mind.

Joe McCarthy, the respected manager of the Chicago Cubs and a man known as a strict disciplinarian, was fired when the Cubs failed to win the 1930 National League pennant, and Ruppert quickly signed him to manage the Yankees for the 1931 season.

Ruth made no secret of the fact that he resented being passed over again as manager, and he was openly hostile to McCarthy from the start. But McCarthy knew there was no profit in getting into a personal feud with Ruth and decided to let him have a free rein while bringing the rest of the team in line. The other players, however, got along well under McCarthy, who indeed brought some order not only into the clubhouse but also into the dugout, hotels, and trains. "You're the Yankees," he kept telling them, trying to instill a sense of class into an unruly mob.

McCarthy insisted all players wear coats and ties when they traveled. He ordered them to shave *before* the games. He forbade card games in the clubhouse. He kept strict curfews when the team was on the road. Only the Babe was exempt from his lectures. Once when Ruth and Jimmie Reese, a rookie player who also liked to have fun on the road, reported late for a game, McCarthy looked past Ruth and barked, "Reese, where have you been?"

Ruth never missed an opportunity to criticize McCarthy's managing, but no one can accuse him of not giving everything he had. He was hitting .400 by the end of June and finished the year batting .373, his highest overall average in seven years. He clouted 46 home runs, drove in 163 runs, and got 199 hits. The Yankees ended up in second place, but it was clear Ruppert intended to keep McCarthy as manager.

At the end of the season, Babe went to California to make some short baseball films, and while he was there he announced that he wanted to play two more years so that he could have twenty years as a player, then he wanted to manage. His two-year contract was up, however, and Ruppert sent him a new one calling for a $10,000 cut in salary.

Babe, who turned thirty-seven in February, was by this time aware that he would have to take a reduced salary. The Depression was in full swing, and almost everybody in baseball was taking pay cuts. Despite his popularity with the fans, which was still helping ticket sales at the box office, he was willing to sign for less. In the end, he and Ruppert found another compromise, and he signed a one-year deal for $75,000.

The 1932 season was the Babe's last great hurrah. Except for two periods—two weeks for a torn muscle in July and another ten days in September with a stomach ailment that landed him in the hospital—he played nearly every day, although he often left the game in the late innings if the Yankees were winning. And the Yankees mostly won that year. They had 107 victories over the season and won the pennant by a wide margin.

By Babe Ruth's standards, it was a respectable year. By anyone else's standards it was a great one. He batted .341 for the season and had 41 home runs. He scored 120 runs and had 137 RBIs. Still, the illness that had forced him into the hospital in September left him weak as the World Series approached. When he returned to batting practice, he was unable to hit a single ball into the stands. But this would be the Babe's tenth World Series and he was not going to miss it, even if he had to play on crutches.

The Yankees faced the Chicago Cubs, and they easily won the first two games at Yankee Stadium before the Series moved back to the Windy City. The Cubs' fans were so rabidly anti-Yankee, particularly anti-Ruth, that the Chicago police had to escort the New York team everywhere they went. And that didn't prevent some fans from spitting on Babe and Claire outside their hotel.

When the Yankees took the field for warm-ups before the third game, some of the fifty thousand fans who had jammed Wrigley Field threw lemons at Babe. Obviously enjoying it all, he picked them up and threw them back. The game didn't begin well for Chicago. In the first inning, an error and a walk had put two men on base when Ruth came up to bat. The first two pitches were balls, and Babe wondered if they were going to walk him intentionally. But that would load the bases, with Gehrig coming to the plate. The next pitch was a low fastball, and Babe drove a home run into the right-field bleachers. The Yankees led 3–0 before a single out was made.

The Cubs fought back to tie the game 4–4 by the fifth inning. Ruth was due to bat second in the inning, and as he stood in the on-deck circle, more lemons came flying out of the stands. The raucous behavior of the crowd had by now spread to the teams, and the players were razzing one another as well. When Ruth stepped to the plate with one out, the entire Cub bench was on the steps of the dugout, calling him names. It was one of the most legendary at bats Ruth had in his entire career and one that has as many different versions as there were witnesses to it.

A pitcher by the name of Charlie Root was on the mound for the Cubs, and he threw the first pitch by the Babe for called strike one. The Cubs and the fans cheered and hurled epithets at Ruth. The Babe stood there, grinning, and held one finger up in the air. The next two pitches were balls—one inside and one outside. The crowd noise quieted considerably, but the next pitch was again over the center of the plate for called strike two, and the hooting and yelling reached a new crescendo. The Babe, still grinning, held up two fingers, turned to the Cubs' catcher and said, "It only takes one to hit it."

Then the Babe either did or did not point his bat to center field. The next pitch became famous as the called shot, but there has always been some confusion about whether Ruth actually called the shot.

There is certainly no confusion over what happened next, however. Root threw a curve ball that tailed low and away, and Ruth swung with all his might. The ball took off like a rocket and kept climbing, and the Cubs' center fielder could only watch it soar over his head into the stands for a home run.

Ruth ran around the bases, laughing all the way. As he crossed third base and headed for home, he raised his clasped hands above his head, like a prizefighter who had just scored a knockout, and, still laughing, was mobbed by his Yankee teammates.

Serious arguments have arisen over the years about whether Ruth actually aimed his bat at center field. There was, of course, no instant replay at the time to settle the argument. All that exists are the accounts of the people who were there.

The legend began with one New York newspaper account the following day that said "Ruth pointed to center" before hitting the ball there. Within days a columnist and two other sportswriters said that Ruth, indeed, had pointed with his bat exactly where he was going to hit his homer. The Cubs' pitcher and catcher both denied he ever pointed to the stands, but it's doubtful they would admit it even if they had seen it.

Ruth himself gave various accounts. Ford Frick, a sportswriter who later became baseball commissioner, once asked him about it. Ruth coyly replied, "It's in the papers, isn't it?" Yes, Frick said, but asked again, "Did you really point to the stands?" "Why don't you read the papers?" Babe said. "It's all right there in the papers." In his autobiography, Ruth said he did call the shot. But he also had the wrong inning and the wrong pitch count for when it happened. Memories are tricky.

Whether he called it or not, it was one of the most dramatic of all the Babe's home runs, and it proved the winning margin in the third game of the Series. The coda to Ruth's legend came on the very next pitch that Root, the Cubs' pitcher, threw. Gehrig stepped up to the plate after Ruth's famous clout and drove a line drive into the left-field stands for back-to-back homers. The Yankees won the fourth game 13–6 for another sweep in the Babe's tenth World Series.

If he had left the game after that World Series he would have been on top of the baseball world. But he wanted to play one more season to give him twenty years in the major leagues. And he still kept hoping that the Yankees would make him their manager when he left the game as a player.

Ruth knew he would have to take another salary cut for the 1933 season, but even he was surprised when Ruppert offered him a contract at $50,000, a reduction of one-third from what he had made the previous year. Babe again tried to negotiate with the Yankee owner, but this time Ruppert was firm. For one thing, the Depression was worse than ever, and there was no money to meet Babe's demands. Ruth kept coming down in his asking price, but the Yankee owner stuck with his offer of $50,000. Finally the Babe accepted Ruppert's figure, but the Yankee owner threw in an extra $2,000 at the end as a gift. Babe was again earning what he had once held out for—a grand a week.

It was clear from opening day that Ruth's power as a player was gone. He was thirty-nine years old and his hard living had caught up with him. He rarely played a whole game, and his batting average dropped like a rock, though he still hit .301 on the year.

There were a couple of moments of glory in the season. In July, the two leagues played the first All-Star Game, and Ruth was included in the American League lineup, as much out of recognition for his past exploits as for anything he was doing that year. In the third inning, however, he hit a home run—the first in an All-Star Game—with two men on, and that proved to be the American League's winning margin in a 4–3 victory.

Then, in the last game of the season, with the Yankees destined to finish second in the standings, Ruth pitched a final game. The Yankees were playing his old team, the Red Sox, and the decision was as much a publicity stunt as anything else. Ruth, however, took the assignment seriously and worked on his pitching for days before the game. After all, he had pitched only once in the past twelve years.

To everyone's surprise, probably including his own, he went the distance and beat the Red Sox 6–5. He gave up 12 hits in the game, but 11 of them were for singles. He got into trouble only once. With the Yankees leading 6–0 in the sixth, he gave up five hits in a row and Boston scored four runs. But McCarthy left him in, and Ruth stopped the rally and finished a complete game. The Babe even hit a home run, which again proved the winning margin. Babe's winning the game meant he never had a losing season as a pitcher.

Ruth again made a play to become the Yankee manager at the end of the year, but Ruppert gave McCarthy another three-year contract. The owner offered to let Ruth manage the Yankee farm team in Newark, New Jersey, but the Babe turned it down. "I'm a big leaguer," he said.

If Ruppert and Barrow thought they would ease the Babe off the field with a job in Newark, he surprised both of them by saying in an interview after an off-season exhibition game: "I'm getting too old. Another year and I'll have to quit."

That remark made the Yankee owner sigh, and he sent Ruth a contract for 1934 calling for a 50 percent pay cut—$25,000. The Babe dutifully complained, and Ruppert in fact increased it to $35,000. Although the glow had gone, Babe Ruth was still a major attraction at ballparks in every city in the league.

Ruth's production fell off dramatically, and although he hit the seven hundredth home run of his career in August, he ended up batting below .300 on the season. His appearances around the league drew large crowds, but there was little doubt in anyone's mind it was a farewell tour. At the end of the season, Ruth made a tour of Japan, where baseball was becoming as much a passion as it was in America, and he sold out stadiums across the country for a series of exhibition games.

The last act in Babe Ruth's career as a baseball player was more like a comic opera than grand drama, and his part resembled that of a clown more than a dashing hero. His countless fans and admirers always wondered why he tried it, and even the Babe admitted later, "It was pretty much of a nightmare."

The fiasco began when the Yankee owner offered Ruth a contract for $1 to report to training camp, and if he made the team, his salary for the rest of the year would then be negotiated. It was a huge insult to the greatest player ever to step on a baseball diamond, and Ruth naturally balked.

At the same time, a former New York judge named Emil Fuchs bought the lowly Boston Braves, a franchise destined to post the worst season record in National League history, worse even than the 1962 Mets. Fuchs was looking for any attraction that would put fans in the Braves' stadium, and he heard that Ruth was available.

After a couple of phone calls to Ruppert, Fuchs offered Ruth a contract with the Braves, hinting broadly that he might become a player-manager with the Braves. Ruth was forty years old, seriously overweight, and starting his twenty-second year in the major leagues.

On opening day, Babe hit a home run, but in the days that followed he couldn't seem to buy a hit. As he wrote in his autobiography: "For the first time in my life, baseball was drudgery. . . . The harder I tried the worse I did."

By May, Ruth was batting .200, and he asked Fuchs not to play him anymore. But the Braves owner talked him into staying in the lineup through the next road trips, and Ruth agreed. There was one more glorious day, playing in Pittsburgh, when Babe hit three home runs in one game. But that was his swan song.

"I wish I had had sense enough to call it a career after this grand and glorious day," Babe wrote in his autobiography. But Fuchs again talked him into staying. By the end of May, he was batting .181. On May 30, 1935, he started the opening game of a holiday doubleheader, but he got a charley horse running for a ball and took himself out after a few innings. He also had a cold.

He sat on the bench for a few games, then decided to quit. He was about to go into Fuchs's office to tell the Braves owner, when some reporters rushed into the dressing room to tell him he had been fired from the team.

"It was quite an ending," the Babe wrote later.

The following year, the Baseball Hall of Fame was established in Cooperstown, New York, and Babe Ruth was one of the five original players voted into it, along with Ty Cobb, Honus Wagner, Christy Mathewson, and Walter Johnson. Although he was out of uniform, he was still the biggest name in baseball.

TEN

IT IS ALMOST impossible to exaggerate the place Babe Ruth occupies in American lore, not only in baseball but also in the national psyche. His very name is synonymous with greatness. A top salesman may find himself called "the Babe Ruth of salesmen." A favorite teacher might earn the appellation "the Babe Ruth of teachers." Enrico Caruso was once referred to as "the Babe Ruth of tenors", and Willie Sutton, the famous outlaw, was once called "the Babe Ruth of bank robbers."

In baseball, a full century after he first stepped on a diamond at St. Mary's Industrial School, Babe Ruth is still the zenith to which every child who picks up a bat and a glove aspires.

During his career, the Babe held a total of fifty-four major-league records, and although most of them have been broken by now—including home runs, in a season (60) and a career (714), and some World Series marks—many held up for decades, until after the ball was hardened and the season was extended by eight games.

The ball that was used when the Babe started out was little more than a piece of leather tightly bound around a cork center. It was pepped up in 1927, and again in 1947, each time to give it a harder core so the ball would carry farther. When the ball was first changed, some sportswriters called it the jackrabbit ball. Babe once commented, "If they put some of the jack in it around 1927, they put the entire rabbit into it in 1947."

Also, by the time Roger Maris first broke the Babe's single-season home run record with 61 in 1961, the teams were playing a 162-game schedule instead of the 154 games teams played in Ruth's day.

During his playing career, his escapades off the field were nearly as famous as his exploits on the diamond.

He could be a clown. Once in an exhibition game

in Florida, Ping Bodie, his first Yankee roommate, cut in front of him to grab a ground ball Ruth was waiting to field. Babe pretended to be angry and picked Ping up, turned him upside down, dropped him on the infield grass, and sat on him. The fans loved it.

He was full of mischief and loved to play practical jokes. He liked to razz his opponents, and sometimes his own teammates. But he could also take teasing from other players. Usually. If he thought some of the barbs—from either players or the fans—were personal, he would go after the heckler and threaten to punch him in the nose.

His antics offended some players, and they would gloat when he struck out or got into trouble with owners, managers, or league officials over his behavior. He could be gross and offensive; he could be thoughtless and crude; he could be abusive and quick to start a fight. But he was just as quick to forget a beef and throw an arm around someone's shoulder. He could be generous and forgiving, and he never stayed mad for long.

For his excellent biography of Ruth, *Babe: The Legend Comes to Life*, Robert W. Creamer talked to two early teammates of Ruth, neither of whom had any particular reason to be overly fond of the Babe. Ernie Shore had been one of Ruth's first teammates—with the Orioles and the Red Sox—and the pitcher who was credited with Ruth for throwing a "combined no-hitter" in 1917. Shore had even roomed with Ruth until they had a dispute over the Babe using Shore's shaving brush. Yet Shore told Creamer: "He was the best-hearted fellow who ever lived. He'd give you the shirt off his back."

Bob Shawkey, another pitcher and a Yankee teammate who managed the team for one season after Miller Huggins death, was the opposite of Ruth in just about every way—a gentle, easygoing player who was never a troublemaker or loudmouth. Creamer asked him why some people disliked Ruth so much. Shawkey looked surprised. "People sometimes got mad at him," Shawkey said. "But I never heard of anybody who didn't *like* Babe Ruth."

Babe's big, moon-shaped, snub-nosed face was so often in the newspapers, that even in those days before television, everyone recognized him wherever he went. Whatever he did was headline news.

Several times during his career, Ruth was reported dead—killed in one of the many auto accidents he had, or from the numerous injuries and illnesses that landed him in the hospital, once even from an airplane crash.

He was famous for not being able to remember names. To compensate for it, he called everybody "kid," which he pronounced "keed." Or "doc," to older men, entitled to more respect. "Hiya, kid" was his greeting to people he had known for years as well as strangers he had just met.

Once, an elderly man with a small boy in tow came up to him in a hotel lobby to ask for an autograph for the boy. Babe reached for his pen. "Sure, kid," he said.

"Who are you calling a 'kid,' me or the boy?" the old man asked.

"The boy," Babe said.

"'Cause I'm old enough to be your granddad," the man explained.

"You got that right, kid," Ruth replied.

There are so many tall tales and stories about Ruth's exploits that it's hard to tell what is fact and what is fiction.

One of the legends about Babe Ruth that was no myth and could not be exaggerated or denied was his love of children. Throughout his career, the Babe made so many visits to orphanages and hospitals to visit children, it is impossible to count them. He spent probably, on average, an hour a day signing autographs. Many players would sign autographs after a game, but it was usually only for those kids at the front of a crowd, and it was the big kids who pushed their way to the front while the little kids got shoved to the back. "Ruth signed for all of them," one former teammate recalled. "He made sure the little ones got autographs, too."

Early on, he would often take reporters with him on those visits to orphanages and hospitals because he thought the kids would like to see stories and pictures of themselves with him in the newspapers. Later, when he was accused of making the visits only for the publicity, he stopped taking reporters. But he didn't stop the visits.

One story became so famous that it served as an example of the Babe's humanity or his lack of it, depending on which version one heard. It involved a boy named Johnny Sylvester. The myth had it that

Johnny was dying in a hospital when the Babe visited him and promised to hit a home run for him that day. He did, and it so thrilled Johnny that he had a miraculous recovery.

In fact, Johnny was in a hospital, bedridden, and doctors thought some emotional stimulation would prompt him to sit up and use his legs again. Johnny was a huge fan of the Babe's, and his father called the Yankees and asked if he might get an autographed baseball. Ruth found out and went to see the boy. He promised to hit a home run for him. And he did, and Johnny got better.

A year later, as the story goes, a man came up to Babe in Philadelphia, introduced himself as Johnny Sylvester's uncle, and thanked him for what he did.

"How's Johnny?" Babe asked.

The man replied that he was fine and everything was okay.

"Good," Babe said. "Give him my regards."

When he left, Babe turned to a sportswriter and asked, "Who is Johnny Sylvester?"

In fact, Ruth, as was his habit, just didn't remember the boy's name. When reminded of the episode, he remembered Johnny well. In fact, Sylvester fully recovered and served in the navy during World War II. He and Ruth kept in touch over the years, and Johnny even visited the Babe in the hospital during his last illness.

Throughout the rest of his life, Ruth nursed some hope that he would end up managing a ball club one day. But the call never came.

In 1938, Babe and Claire went to see the first major-league night game played in New York at Ebbets Field, the new home of the Brooklyn Dodgers. The fans stood and cheered and gave him such a welcome when he arrived, the Dodgers' owners decided he would help their box office if they could get him in a uniform, so they offered him a job as a coach on the team.

Ruth accepted, and he spent the last half of the season trotting out to the coach's box in a Dodgers' uniform. His presence did attract more fans for the Brooklyn team, but when Leo Durocher, one of the few men in baseball who genuinely disliked Ruth, became manager the following season, he didn't bring Babe back as coach.

In 1939, Ruppert died and his estate sold the Yankees to a syndicate headed by Larry MacPhail. In the Babe's last attempt at managing, he phoned MacPhail and asked if he could manage the Newark farm team—the same job he turned down years earlier. MacPhail said he would think it over and get back in touch. But he never called.

On July Fourth that same year, Ruth put on his old Yankee uniform for an appearance he wished hadn't been necessary. Lou Gehrig had been diagnosed with a rare muscular disease that was forcing the player once known as the Iron Horse, because of his record 2,130 straight games, to retire and soon would take his life at the age of thirty-seven. The illness, amyotrophic lateral sclerosis, would become known as Lou Gehrig's disease, after its most famous victim. The Yankees were honoring him with a special day.

Ruth and Gehrig had once been best friends. Ruth often visited Gehrig's house, and he was a big favorite of Ma Gehrig, who would cook up immense portions of the Babe's favorite dishes. Later, however, after Gehrig married, there was a falling-out. The cause was never very clear, although it was reported to be over a disparaging remark Ma Gehrig once made about Claire's clear preference for her own daughter, Julia, over Dorothy. In fact, Dorothy and Claire never got along well, and Dorothy left home when she turned eighteen, although she remained close to Ruth all his life. At the time, Babe said something to Lou about Ma Gehrig minding her own business, and Gehrig took umbrage at that. At any rate, the two men were always respectful but distant after the feud.

On that Independence Day, Ruth and other former and present players stood near home plate while Gehrig made his famous farewell speech, in which he said that despite his debilitating illness, "I consider myself to be the luckiest man on the face of the earth." Tears in his eyes, Ruth went over to his old friend, and the two men embraced at home plate, whatever feud had once separated them now forgotten.

Babe made a few other appearances. During World War II, he put on his uniform again for a benefit at Yankee Stadium and batted against Walter Johnson. He also did some work for the Red Cross during the war.

Late in 1946, Babe, now fifty-one years old, began to have sharp pains over his left eye, and he entered the French Hospital in New York for tests. Doctors found a malignant tumor in his neck, and he underwent an operation. The surgeons could not remove all of it, and he was given radiation treatment. Ruth stayed in the hospital three months and lost eighty pounds. After he was discharged, he went to Florida to recuperate. He played a little golf and went fishing, but he was only a shell of his former self.

On Sunday, April 27, 1947, the new Commissioner of Major League Baseball, Happy Chandler, decreed Babe Ruth Day throughout the major leagues, and a ceremony honoring the Babe's contributions to baseball was held in every city. The biggest, of course, was at Yankee Stadium, and when Ruth walked out onto the diamond, thin and weak, the sixty thousand fans cheered him wildly.

The Babe, his voice barely a croak, made a speech. "You know how bad my voice sounds," he began. "Well, it feels just as bad." He saluted the youth of America and thanked the fans for their support and called baseball "the only real game in the world."

The tumor recurred later that year, and doctors treated him with an experimental drug that gave him some relief and brought a marked improvement in his condition. He traveled some that fall and created the Babe Ruth Foundation to help poor kids. There was another Babe Ruth Day at the stadium in September to raise money for the foundation, and he showed up to watch an old-timers' game with Ty Cobb and Tris Speaker. He had hoped to be strong enough to pitch an inning, but he wasn't.

The following summer, on June 13, 1948, the Yankees celebrated the twenty-fifth anniversary of The House That Ruth Built, and the Babe again put on a uniform and walked out on the diamond. Using

The Babe put on his old uniform and used a bat as a cane for his final farewell at Yankee Stadium on June 13, 1948.

a bat for a cane, he strode out to home plate before a packed Yankee Stadium, and the cheers and applause washed over him.

During his career, no man had been cheered louder by so many fans. And no man had been booed louder, either. The Babe had relished both. But there were nothing but cheers that day. It was the last time he appeared in public.

He was back in the hospital a week later. He left it briefly in July to attend the opening of *The Babe Ruth Story*, a movie about his life that was more fiction than fact, but he had to leave before it was over. He died a month later.

It's been over sixty years since his death, and over seventy-three years since he hit a home run. The House That Ruth Built has been abandoned, and most of his records have been broken. Yet his name is still heard in sandlots and major-league ballparks around the world, a synonym for greatness for the great American pastime.

Babe Ruth was so many different things to so many people, it's impossible to summarize his life. For the Babe, baseball was not just a game but a way of life, and he lived to the fullest. Perhaps the Babe himself delivered his own best epitaph. Once, discussing his batting technique, he said:

> I swing as hard as I can, and I try to swing right through the ball. The harder you grip the bat, the more you can swing it through the ball and the farther the ball will go. I swing big, with everything I've got. I hit big or I miss big. I like to live as big as I can.

SOURCE NOTES

INTRODUCTION

"Ruth can hit" to "he can do anything": Montville, *The Big Bam*, 34.

"had me pitch . . .": Ruth, *Babe Ruth's Own Book of Baseball*, 9.

"How about it" to "Sure . . .": Ruth, *Babe Ruth's Own Book*, 10.

"There goes . . .": Creamer, *Babe*, 52.

CHAPTER ONE

"I was a bad kid": Ruth and Considine, *The Babe Ruth Story*, 11.

"What difference . . .": Creamer, *Babe*, 26.

"We were poor. . . .": *Babe Ruth's Own Book*, 4.

"mainly Irish": Ruth and Considine, *Babe Ruth Story*, 11.

"a convert,": Montville, *Big Bam*, 10.

"in the restaurant . . .": Montville, *Big Bam*, 148.

"I hardly knew . . .": Ruth and Considine, *Babe Ruth Story*, 12.

"mine has only . . .": Creamer, *Babe*, 24.

"exhaustion": Brother Gilbert, *Young Babe Ruth*, 2.

"Pigtown": Montville, *Big Bam*, 9.

"incorrigible": Ruth and Considine, *Babe Ruth Story*, 12.

"parole": Creamer, *Babe*, 32.

CHAPTER TWO

"I think I was born . . .": Ruth and Considine, *Babe Ruth Story*, 15.

"What are you laughing . . ." to ". . . how it's done.": Ruth and Considine, *Babe Ruth Story*, 17.

"I felt, somehow . . .": Ruth and Considine, *Babe Ruth Story*, 17.

"parole": Creamer, *Babe*, 32.

"the rich school . . .": Creamer, *Babe*, 49.

"Clad in a baseball uniform . . ." and "He also struck out . . .": Montville, *Big Bam*, 27.

"the greatest man . . .": Ruth and Considine, *Babe Ruth Story*, 13.

"You'll make it . . .": Ruth and Considine, *Babe Ruth Story*, 21.

CHAPTER THREE

"You mean . . ." to "to play ball": Ruth and Considine, *Babe Ruth Story*, 24.

"The next batter . . ." "Homer by . . ." and "Ruth makes . . .": Creamer, *Babe*, 61.

"He's one of . . .": Montville, *Big Bam*, 36.

"If you want . . .": Creamer, *Babe*, 66.

"He has all . . ." to ". . . ever had.": Creamer, *Babe*, 63.

"We had never . . ." to ". . . batting": Creamer, *Babe*, 69–70.

CHAPTER FOUR

"Who are they . . ." to "your friends?": Creamer, *Babe*, 74.

"You're doing fine . . .": Ruth and Considine, *Babe Ruth Story*, 55.

"Hon, how about . . .": Creamer, *Babe*, 100.

CHAPTER FIVE

"His name is . . .": Creamer, *Babe*, 108.

"All right, we've . . .": Creamer, *Babe*, 121.

"You're a fine . . ." to ". . . your father.": Creamer, *Babe*, 110.

"I'm working on . . .": Creamer, *Babe*, 135.

"I'll bust you . . .": Creamer, *Babe*, 139.

"I'd be the laughingstock . . .": Creamer, *Babe*, 152.

"I quit.": Creamer, *Babe*, 162.

CHAPTER SIX

"You're a fine citizen . . .": Creamer, *Babe*, 193.

"Am I playing . . ." to "further notice.": Creamer, *Babe*, 194.

"Ed, someday . . ." to ". . . been going.": *Babe*, 195.

CHAPTER SEVEN

"I don't know . . ." to ". . . his suitcase.": Creamer, *Babe*, 222.

"every kind of bum . . .": Ruth and Considine, *Babe Ruth Story*, 85.

"To me, it was . . .": Ruth and Considine, *Babe Ruth Story*, 90.

"Oh, you are . . ." to ". . . running this game." and "Tell the old guy . . .": Creamer, *Babe*, 246.

"Make it fifty-two . . ." to ". . . grand a week.": Creamer, *Babe*, 254.

"You big bum . . .": Creamer, *Babe*, 258.

"kids of America.": Montville, *Big Bam*, 158.

CHAPTER EIGHT

"I don't care . . ." to ". . . when he returns": Montville, *Big Bam*, 209.

"the flea": Montville, *Big Bam*, 119.

"I'm burning up . . ." to ". . . body aches.": Creamer, *Babe*, 286.

"the bellyache . . .": Creamer, *Babe*, 289.

"Don't bother getting . . ." to ". . . o'clock train.": Creamer, *Babe*, 292–93.

"I'm through . . .": Creamer, *Babe*, 294.

"I'm behind . . ." and "I guess . . .": Creamer, *Babe*, 296.

"No, he is not . . .": Creamer, *Babe*, 298.

"Yes, of course . . .": Creamer, *Babe*, 299.

"acted like . . ." and "I am not proud . . .": Ruth and Considine, *Babe Ruth Story*, 143.

"Babe, I admire . . ." to ". . . fine back.": Ruth and Considine, *Babe Ruth Story*, 147.

"I really was . . .": Ruth and Considine, *Babe Ruth Story*, 148.

CHAPTER NINE

"I hold nothing . . ." and "I'd rather not . . .": Creamer, *Babe*, 340.

"Why not . . .": Creamer, *Babe*, 351.

"You're the Yankees . . .": Creamer, *Babe*, 353.

"Reese, where . . .": Creamer, *Babe*, 352.

"It only takes one . . .": Creamer, *Babe*, 361.

"Ruth pointed . . .": Creamer, *Babe*, 363.

"It's in . . ." to "in the papers.": Creamer, *Babe*, 368.

"I'm a big-leaguer . . ." and "I'm getting too old . . .": Creamer, *Babe*, 374.

"It was pretty much . . ." and "For the first time . . .": Ruth and Considine, *Babe Ruth Story*, 208.

"I wish I had . . .": Ruth and Considine, *Babe Ruth Story*, 210.

"It was quite . . .": Ruth and Considine, *Babe Ruth Story*, 211.

CHAPTER TEN

"The Babe Ruth of tenors" and "the Babe Ruth of bank . . .": Creamer, *Babe*, 16.

"If they put . . .": Ruth and Considine, *Babe Ruth Story*, 156.

"He was . . ." and "People sometimes . . .": Creamer, *Babe*, 20.

"Sure, kid . . ." to ". . . that right, kid.": Ruth and Considine, *Babe Ruth Story*, 125.

"Ruth signed . . ." to ". . . too.": Creamer, *Babe*, 412.

"How's Johnny?" to ". . . is Johnny Sylvester?": Ruth and Considine, *Babe Ruth Story*, 174.

"I consider myself . . .": Ruth and Considine, *Babe Ruth Story*, 216.

"You know how bad . . ." to ". . . in the world.": Creamer, *Babe*, 419.

"I swing as hard . . .": Creamer, *Babe*, 330–31.

BIBLIOGRAPHY

Creamer, Robert W. *Babe: The Legend Comes to Life*. New York: Simon & Schuster, 1974.

Gilbert, Brother. Edited by Harry Rothgerber. *Young Babe Ruth: His Early Life and Baseball Career from the Memoirs of a Xaverian Brother*. Jefferson, North Carolina: McFarland and Co., 1994.

Montville, Leigh. *The Big Bam: The Life and Times of Babe Ruth*. New York: Doubleday, 2006.

Ruth, George Herman, as told to Bob Considine. *The Babe Ruth Story*. New York: E. P. Dutton & Co., 1948.

———. *Babe Ruth's Own Book of Baseball*. Lincoln, Nebraska: Bison Books/University of Nebraska Press, 1992. (Originally published by P. G. Putnam's Sons, New York, 1928.)

INDEX

Note: Page numbers in *italics* refer to illustrations

PHOTO CREDITS